ESCAPE

FROM

FRANCE

1944

The Secret Forest of Freteval

A true
World War II
escape story

by
Raymond Worrall

This book is dedicated to my wife, Frederica,
with-out whose encouragement
it would not have been written.

Published by
Silver Quill Publications
Silver Quill Limited
Movade House
Catterick
North Yorkshire
DL10 7QF

Tel: 01748 812937

Printed by
The Printers Limited
Movade House
Catterick
North Yorkshire
DL10 7QF

First Edition
Published April 23rd
2004

ISBN No: 1 872939 80 5

*To Michael
& Sheila
with best - wishes.
I hope you find
this book interesting.
Ray*

*Raymond Worrall
Micklethwaite
Wetherby
Jan. 2006*

3

British Library Cataloguing in Publication Data.

A catalogue record for this book is
available from the British Library.

Every effort has been made to check the completeness
and accuracy of the information included in this book.
However during war few have access to all facts and
there may be additional information available.

The author welcomes correspondence from readers.

If you do not know his address
letters sent to Silver Quill Publications
and addressed to Mr R Worrall
will be forwarded unopened.
Further information and detail
will be recorded, if appropriate,
in future editions.

CONTENTS

Foreword by Air Chief Marshal Sir Lewis Hodges

Preface

5

Foreword

by

Air Chief Marshal Sir Lewis Hodges
KCB, CBE, DSO, DFC, DL

The story of the escape from the Freteval Forest, whereby 152 Allied aircrew were hidden under the noses of the Germans, in some cases for as long as three months, is one of the most successful and unique in the annals of clandestine warfare.

Successful it certainly was to have enabled so many airmen to escape unharmed. It was unique in that the airmen consisted of British, American, South African, Australian, New Zealand, and Belgian, who lived in two camps in the middle of occupied France in the Forest of Freteval between Cloyes and Vendome under the shadow of the German occupying troops. These airmen, who had been shot down over enemy territory, were nearly all from Bomber Squadrons.

It was also unique in that this operation entailed the bringing together of many members of the Resistance, and that it remained absolutely secret, secret even to the point that the inhabitants of the villages surrounding the forest were unaware of the existence of Allied airmen so close to them.

The success of the operation was thanks to the cooperation between the British Secret Service, the Royal Air Force and the French Resistance, the collective effort inspired by patriotic and humanitarian impulse.

The silence which had to be respected after the war (as was the case with many secret operations), and the modesty of the many members of the Resistance in the Eure et Loir and Loir et Cher region who took part, prevented the telling of this unique feat. Apart from a few articles in local newspapers from time to time and mostly in France, the story has never been told. Sadly there are only a few now left from those involved to tell the tale.

One such person is the author, Raymond Worrall, who spent three weeks in the Forest of Freteval from the end of July 1944 to the middle of August, after parachuting from his crashing Lancaster in the Chateaudun area, a few miles away. It is a fascinating true story and it deserves to be told.

I commend it to all who are interested in the clandestine warfare of World War Two.

The second part of the book describes the author's experiences in trans-Atlantic flying when he was engaged in delivering aircraft from Canada to Europe and the Far East in the final months of the war.

Air Chief Marshal Sir Lewis Hodges
Sevenoakes
Kent

March 2004

Preface

For some years after the second world war it was forbidden to publicise stories about escape where (as in most cases) the escaper or evader had been helped by a secret underground escape organisation. This was because there was the possibility that such help might be required again at some future time. However, by the 1960's this ban ceased to exist and so, on being invited by Leeds Round Table, (of which I was a member), to give a talk on my experiences in evading capture, I was able to do so.

After the talk I was given £10, a princely sum in those days, as a donation to the Royal Air Force Escaping Society. This gave me the idea of giving further talks to raise money for the RAFES. Thus, since that time I have given almost 150 talks to such organisations as Round Tables, Rotary Clubs, Women's Institutes, Towns Women's Guilds, Church groups and similar organisations. I have raised over £2,500 for the Society and for the RAF Benevolent Fund. Often, after such talks, I was asked if I had written a book, or had I considered having my story printed.

Because of the enormity of the task and the fact that it was easier to talk about it than to write about it, I did not follow up the suggestions made. But in retirement, and with pressure and encouragement from my wife, who wanted to have a record for the family, I got out my word processor and began to type . . . . .

Raymond Worrall
Allandale
Leeds
LS17 7DH

April 2004

All photographs are

by the Author

except for the Crew

taken by a RAF photographer

and the back cover photograph

photographed by the publisher.

Cover Design

by

Suzanne M Thorp

and

Dorian Robinson

Cover graphic artwork

and maps by

Chris Milnes Graphics

Harrogate.

The Crew, from left to right, shortly before their last trip.
Flight Sergeant **Tom Whitehead**, Mid Upper Gunner. Flight Sergeant **Frank Wells**, Rear Gunner.
Sergeant **Ken Andrews**, Wireless operator. Flight Sergeant **Ted Greatz**, Navigator.
Flying Officer **Dudley Ibbotson**, Pilot.
Sergeant **Ray Worrall**, Flight Engineer. Flight Sergeant **Ian Murray**, Bomb Aimer.

IT BEGAN IN 1943.

Chapter one

In January 1943 I joined the RAF as an aircrew flight engineer. I was a volunteer and like a lot of others who joined up at this time, we wanted to be pilots, but at this stage of the war there were sufficient pilots in training and there was a bottle neck on the courses. On the other hand with the advent of the four engined bomber force there was a shortage of flight engineers and we were encouraged to remuster. With the prospect of delayed entry and then of spending a lot of time in transit camps in between different stages of pilot training, it was an incentive to remuster and get on with the job which many of us did. As flight engineers, apart from a few who went to Coastal or Transport Commands, we were destined for Bomber Command.

During the Second World War, RAF Bomber Command flew more than a third of a million sorties during the course of which 55,000 airmen were killed and 18,000 wounded, or became prisoners of war. Over one third of all these casualties occurred in 1944, a year that opened with the concluding phase of the Battle of Berlin and the costly Nuremberg raid. 1944 also saw a change in policy and a move away from area bombing to the more tactical targets such as rail centres, troop concentrations and gun sites as a prelude to and a follow up from the invasion of the European mainland by the Allied forces. Bomber Command also contributed to the attacks on the V1 launching sites.

The work of Bomber Command during the war of 1939-1945 is best known in the eyes of the public for the headline exploits such as the Dam Busters raid on the Mohne and Eder dams, the Thousand Bomber Raids, the Nuremberg Raid, the sinking of the Tirpitz and for its heroes such as Guy Gibson VC and Leonard Cheshire VC. However the vast majority of the operations carried out by Bomber Command were less spectacular and did not reach the headlines. Nevertheless danger was ever present not only from anti-aircraft fire and German fighters but also with bad weather to contend with en route or over base on return, with none of the sophisticated equipment with which modern aircraft are equipped. Further with large numbers of aircraft converging over a small target there was always the danger of mid air collisions. They suffered from loneliness, fear and the nervous strain of operating in the air, and the air gunners from intense cold in their turrets. Most crews consisted of ordinary chaps who tried to do their best from what they had been taught to do, during their long period of training.

Aircrews of Bomber Command, contrary to popular belief, were not dauntless dare-devils thirsting for action, and they disliked what seemed occasionally to be a tacit assumption that they were effortlessly gallant and irresponsibly "devil may care" as to be insensitive to all but the immediate present, and indifferent to their own ultimate fate. For each man there was a constant awareness of danger from the enemy, from the sudden blinding of searchlights accompanied by heavy and accurate flak, from packs of night fighters seeking to penetrate the bomber stream, of danger from collision, from ice in the cloud, a hit in the petrol tank causing loss of fuel resulting in an explosion or a forced landing in the sea on the way back. There was no single moment of security from take off to landing, but often the sight of other aircraft hit by flak and exploding in the air or plummeting down blazing to strike the ground in a ball of fire. The chances of any individual surviving his thirty trips alive, un-wounded, and without having been taken prisoner or having been forced down over enemy territory were generally accepted as being one in five. This caused a definite nervous toll on a man. The first two or three sorties were so full of novelty and excitement that unless a man was fundamentally unsuited to operational flying, he would not suffer from actual fear, to any great extent. But by the time he had completed from five to eight sorties he had discovered the danger and magnitude of the job, which he had undertaken. The extreme novelty of the operations had gone to be replaced by a growing recognition of the cost. By the twelfth or fifteenth sortie he had reached a full realisation of the danger and unpleasantness of the job he had undertaken, and the long stretch of sorties still before him. As the tour continued morale rose until by the twenty fifth trip the cumulative stress and fatigue began to tell and morale fell during the last few sorties. So much so that when, on our twenty sixth trip, we had to bale out from about 10,000 feet, afterwards, talking to Ted our navigator, he told me that when his parachute opened he burst into uncontrollable laughter at 8,000 feet or so, due to nervous reaction on finding himself alive, because by that stage he was convinced he was not going to finish his tour of thirty operations alive.

Six out of the seven members of the crew of which I became part lived to tell the tale but most of our comrades did not, shattered by gun fire or desperately trying to find the escape hatch in a falling bomber, or drowning in a stricken aircraft which failed to return, or being caught up in an exploding bomber as it hit the ground, or often in the case of an air gunner bleeding to death, trapped in a lonely gun turret.

At the beginning of February 1943 on a cold, damp, dreary winter's morning I reported to my first unit, the aircrew receiving centre at St John's Wood London. We were then billeted in blocks of luxury flats which had been built and finished at the outbreak of the war but had not been occupied when the RAF took them over. Stripped of their luxury fittings they made very good billets. On the first day we stood about for hours and then we filled in forms, had our photographs taken and were kitted out with our uniform. After that we had our medicals, inoculations and we attended lectures.

After three weeks I was posted to ITW (Initial Training Wing) at Bridlington, the well-known Yorkshire resort, but this was to be no holiday. We were woken up at 6am to be marched off for breakfast. On parade at 7am with square bashing on the sea front with a February wind blowing off the North Sea. After that the day was spent marching from one lecture hall to another to attend lectures on aircraft recognition, navigation, the Kings Regulations, morse code as well as rifle drill and PT.

After about eight weeks we were posted to St Athan, a large pre war RAF station near Cardiff. The station was very well equipped with amenities such as a gym, swimming pool and a large cinema which doubled as a concert hall, in which concerts were often given by famous artists and orchestras such as The BBC Symphony Orchestra. At St Athan we learned all about aircraft and aircraft engines. We were given lectures on both radial and inline engines, their parts and functions, lubrication, fuel supply, ignition, superchargers, electrical systems, instruments, cooling systems, hydraulics, pneumatics, propellers etc. There was much to learn about the Rolls Royce Merlin engine in particular, not only its construction and constituent parts, but its operation and working limitations under various conditions and most importantly how to adjust boost and revs to obtain maximum fuel economy with maximum power.

By the end of November the course completed, I passed the necessary tests and examinations went on the passing out parade and found myself posted to RAF Scampton a famous Bomber Command station near Lincoln. It was from here that the Dambusters had taken off on their famous raid. However at the time Scampton was not operational. It was being upgraded. In particular concrete runways were being laid to replace the grass runways. In the interim, therefore, it was being used as an aircrew commando school where we attended more lectures to prepare us for the demands which would be placed upon us on a bomber squadron, including some on escape and evasion. We were fortunate enough to be given leave for Christmas, and then soon after my return I was posted to RAF Winthorpe where I met six others who were to form the crew. There was no formal way of selecting crews to fly with each other it was done by mixing together in the Sergeants Mess, or in the flight offices, and then joining a crew with whom one felt most comfortable. The crew I joined composed Flight Sergeant Ibbotson the pilot and skipper, " Ibby to his crew", a steady and level headed Australian, aged twenty five, Sergeant Ted Greatz, navigator, Sergeant Ian Murray, bomb aimer, also Australians, Sergeant Ken Andrews, wireless operator, Sergeant Tom Whitehead, mid upper gunner, all in their early twenties and Sergeant Frank Wells, rear gunner, who at thirty three was the oldest. I was then aged nineteen.

RAF Winthorpe was a heavy conversion unit for the purpose of training air crew to fly four engined bombers. It was equipped with Short Stirlings which

15

were obsolete so far as operational duties were concerned because they were too slow and unable to fly high enough, and therefore an easy target for enemy fighters and anti aircraft guns. At Winthorpe we learned to fly the Stirling. We practised take offs and landings (circuits and bumps); we did cross country flying by day and by night, and we practised evasive tactics. As we would be graduating on to Lancasters on which the flight engineer had to take the place of a second pilot (there was no second pilot on any of the four engined bombers), I had to do training on the link trainer, now called a flight simulator. Stirlings were becoming obsolete. We also did bombing practice out to sea off the Lincolnshire coast. On all these occasions except towards the end of the course the pilot and flight engineer were accompanied by an experienced pilot and flight engineer who had completed a tour of operations.

After about eight weeks we were posted to RAF Syerston near Nottingham. This was a Lancaster finishing school. This was because we were marked for a Lancaster Squadron, a very different aircraft from the Stirling, and we had to familiarise ourselves with it. Then after another month or so we were posted as a crew to No 44 Squadron at Dunholme Lodge, a wartime bomber station built in the early years of the war. It was a Nissen hutted camp, spread out so that one had to do a lot of walking to get from one section to another. It was designated as a Rhodesian squadron, although there were very few Rhodesians on it, most of the aircrew being English, Australian and Canadian.

INTO THE BREACH

Chapter two

We arrived at Dunholme Lodge just in time for lunch on 31 March 1944 about to start the luckiest period of my life. Over the following 5 months I had luck, which I can only compare to winning the lottery. On entering the Sergeant's Mess the atmosphere was cold and unfriendly; little was said. When the 1 o'clock news came on the radio we discovered the reason. The squadron had taken part the previous night in the Nuremberg raid, one of Bomber Command's disasters. Of the 795 aircraft despatched ninety four were shot down and many others were severely damaged. What happened, during the eight hours or so that it took the crews to complete the round journey, is etched forever in the history of the Royal Air Force. The German night fighters infiltrated the bomber stream all the way from the Belgian coast to Nuremberg and were fitted with two 20mm cannon guns firing upwards at an angle 60 to 70 degrees, and using non tracer ammunition they exacted a heavy toll on the unsuspecting bombers, who never knew what had hit them. If we had been posted to the squadron a few days earlier we would have taken part in that disastrous raid.

We were arriving on an operational squadron at a dangerous time, and also an interesting time, since new bombing techniques were getting under way. By the spring of 1943 it would have been prohibitive if the bomber force had had to continue to carry out its major operations in moonlight and clear weather in order to see the target. Two new devices which were coming into use, although still in short supply, made fog haze and low cloud no longer an obstacle. The two new devices were known by their code names, Oboe and H2S. Oboe was based on signals transmitted from ground stations and was used for accurate target finding, marking and bombing by radar. H2S, the other device, involved no transmission from ground stations. The transmission was from the aircraft itself and this was echoed back to the aircraft in such a way as to give a fairly clear picture of certain features on the ground, particularly built-up areas and coastlines. Since there were no ground stations involved H2S could be used at any range and any number of aircraft could use it at the same time, whereas Oboe could only be used to guide very few aircraft at a time. As against this H2S was much less accurate than bombing by Oboe. As Oboe could only be used by very few aircraft at a time it was fitted to Pathfinder Mosquitoes who would then identify the target on Oboe. They then dropped coloured flare markers which dangled above the target, so that they could be used as aiming points, by the main force which followed and aimed at these "Sky Markers." As these flares could be seen through cloud bombing could be done through cloud. A great advantage from hitherto. This technique became known as sky marking.

Oboe ground marking was also developed. This was similar, but the target was marked with coloured markers on the ground, and the accuracy was then checked by controllers in Mosquitoes flying low over the target. These were sometimes backed up with sky markers of a different colour depending on visibility.

With this background in mind we were briefed for our first operation on 26 April. The target was Schweinfurt. The object to destroy the ball bearing works. We were soon to become accustomed to the normal operational procedure. Down at the flight offices we were told to report for briefing which always took place about two hours before take off. Crews assembled for briefing, pilots, navigators and bomb aimers received information about the target, its location distinguishing features, flight path, altitude, enemy defences en route and over the target, Weather details included cloud cover, wind direction and speed, and general weather conditions. Other members of the crew had their own briefing after which all crew members assembled for final briefing when we would be given final details including what to do in an emergency, such as of friendly territory, where a damaged aircraft could be set down and how to contact escape organisations if one was shot down and had the good fortune to reach the ground alive. Then the final order; synchronise your watches. After "good luck" from the Station and Squadron commanders we were released, full of apprehension, as to what the next few hours would bring.

All crews then went to the aircrew dining hall where we were given egg and chips, a luxury in wartime Britain. After the meal we went to the locker room to divest ourselves of all personal possessions. Parachutes and Mae Wests (life jackets) were then collected and the air gunners, who were subjected to extreme cold even in the summer, wore over their battledress a kapok inner suit and a canvas outer suit which was electrically heated. The rest of the crew did not need such cumbersome clothing because the cabin heating in a Lancaster was very efficient. Then crew by crew we were transported each crew to our own aircraft which was standing ready at the dispersal point on the airfield. Beside the aircraft the ground crew waited for us to go through the numerous checks which were necessary before the Lancaster, now fully fuelled armed and serviced and loaded with bombs, could be officially handed over to the skipper. The skipper and flight engineer walked round and under the aircraft to check that the various covers were off and the panels secure. There was a standard routine to be followed. Pitot head cover off, chocks under the wheels, tyres undamaged, leading edges secure, all cowlings and inspection panels secure, ensure the correct hydraulic leg extension on the undercarriage, check for any leaks of coolant or oil. Then fins, rudders, tailplane, elevators, and ailerons undamaged. In so far as the pitot head was concerned airflow in and through the pitot head was crucial because the different air pressures created in it were essential for operating the airspeed indicator, and therefore to leave the canvas cover on would be fatal.

We then climbed into the aircraft by the rear door. The skipper and flight engineer continued their checks such as all fire extinguishers and first aid kits in place, axe secure, portable oxygen sets in position secure and operating, bomb slip covers secure, pyrotechnics in place, roof escape hatches secure, oxygen main cock turned on, emergency air pressure at 1,200 lbs per sq in, hydraulic accumulator pressure correct, fuel cross feed cock off, ground to flight switch to flight, all negative earthing switches in main fuse panel ON, turn fuel contents gauge to ON, and check contents, test booster pumps and prime carburettors, check brakes functioning. It was a lengthy list but it had to be done as a matter of routine. By this time the pilot was settled in his seat and checking the flying controls while the engineer was scanning his own control panel and its gauges. Meanwhile, the rest of the crew having completed their own checks, were taking up their own positions and putting on flying helmets and plugging into the intercom. By this time the engines were ready to be started with the assistance of the ground crew who had already plugged in the external accumulator on a trolley under the starboard inner engine to supply the initial power to turn the mighty Rolls Royce Merlin engine.

Inside the pilot and engineer complete another set of checks, seting `Ground to Flight' switch to `Ground', selected no 2 fuel tank, undercarriage lever down, flap control neutral, bomb doors closed, flap switch and undercarriage warning lights on, air intake set at cold, master fuel cocks off, no 2 tank booster pumps on, supercharger in "M" gear, throttles half-inch open, propeller controls fully up, booster coil and ignition switches on, turn on the master fuel cock for the appropriate engine, and then thumbs up to the ground crew below. Contact and press the starter button while the ground crew mechanic standing on the wheel primes the engine in the nacelle. The propeller slowly turns then the engine coughs and a puff of smoke comes from the exhaust outlets on each side before running smoothly with some adjustment of the throttles. The trolley is disconnected since the generator on the starboard engine can now give the power to start up the others. As each engine is started the various services on the aircraft come into operation and from the generators and pumps come the power and the pressures to operate the electrical and hydraulic equipment. Pressures and temperatures are tested and checked as the engines are run up. Gunners rotate their turrets and check the operation of their guns. The navigator twiddles the knobs of his Gee and H2S sets and the wireless operator finds his wavelengths. All crew members are busy in their various jobs and call out OK or report problems if they have any. When all the crew have done their checks the skipper signed form 600, and the aircraft then became his sole responsibility!

The Very light from flying control alerted us for take off. All around the airfield propellers were beginning to turn as other aircraft stuttered into life and filled the air with noise. Final checks redone before taxing out to the runway, `Ground to Flight' switch set to `Flight', navigation lights on or off as required, main auto control switch Off, DR compass switches On and to setting, set altimeter, check undercarriage warning light change over switch, test oxygen and intercom again and check brake pressure. "All OK rear gunner"? "OK Skipper"; "mid-upper gunner"? "OK Skipper". Down the aircraft come the responses. Thumbs up to the ground crew who move in to remove the wheel chocks. The release of the brake lever on the control column brings a hiss and the aircraft slowly moves out of dispersal to taxy around the perimeter track towards the end of the runway. Converging at that point are the other aircraft detailed for the attack, rudders wagging as the pilots steer the heavy Lancasters to take up station one behind the other in a long queue. One by one the Lancasters get the Aldis signal from the caravan at the end of the runway and move slowly forward and swing on to the runway. A further range of checks around the cockpit, Auto-control clutch IN auto controls OUT, pitot head heater ON, trimming tabs-elevator slightly forward, rudder and aileron neutral, boost control not pulled, propeller pitch FULLY FINE, fuel master cocks ON, tank selector cocks to no 2 and all booster pumps ON, air intake COLD, FLAPS 25% brake pressure 130 lbs per sq inch.

The Lancaster moves forward resisting slightly because of the heavy load. We stop at the caravan, a few more checks then the Aldis lamp from the caravan flashes green, the engines are opened up to zero boost against the brakes. The engineer calls out pressures and temperatures. "All OK Skipper," who replies "OK, lets go". The Skipper moves the throttles slowly forward manipulating them to keep the aircraft straight as the speed and the power increase. The navigator calls the speed and the engineer takes control of the four throttles and takes them through `the gate' to give 3,000 revs and full boost. The aircraft slowly lifts off the runway, the pilot calls "wheels up", the engineer replies "wheels up skipper". Ease off flap, climbing power engineer .
. .   throttle back to 2,850 revs and 9lbs boost and the engineer reports climbing power as the operation begins. The manipulation of the engines continue and pilot, engineer and navigator frequently exchange instructions and information in order to conform to the flight plan. It was important to have regular disciplined communication between crew members.

Our first trip was a difficult and dangerous one. The target was Schweinfurt, a small German industrial town considered to be of great importance as the centre of Germany's ball bearing industry. It was known to be heavily defended, not only by flak and search lights, but by a smoke screen and the use of decoys. The attack was carried out in very difficult circumstances. We were routed southwards across France as if making for Italy as in an attack on Munich two nights before, but this time the ploy did not work and the enemy had conserved his fighters in expectation of just such an attack on

Southern Germany, as in fact it was. Further, the weather helped the night fighters because at the last moment the wind changed direction and increased by 10 mph. This delayed the main marker force which had taken the indirect route, like the main force, to deceive the Germans.

On the other hand the Mosquitoes of the initial marker force took the direct route and further helped by a favourable wind arrived at the target well before the main marking force which was late. This caused a delay in the marking of the target. Consequently when we in the main force arrived over the target the marking indicators had not gone down, and it was necessary to orbit the target (ie. circle the target) until the indicators had gone down, and had been assessed by the controller, before he could give us the order to go in and bomb. This was always a dangerous situation because it gave the enemy time to get his fighters up and his defences into action. Also there was ever present the danger of mid air collisions.

After an anxious time in orbit the words of the controller crackled over the RT. "Main force go in and bomb". We bombed from 15,500 feet. In my position up beside the pilot I had my first sight of a target, of which many were to follow. Looking down my fear was partly diverted by the novelty of what I was witnessing. For the first time I was actually doing what I had joined up to do and what previously I had only read about in the papers and heard about on the wireless. I found myself looking down on a great firework display, many fires were burning and lighting up the target. Coloured target indicators were going down, flak was coming up, search lights were sweeping the sky looking for us, and aircraft were going down in flames. There were night fighters about and bombs from an aircraft above us were dropped, and just missed hitting us.

We flew on a steady and level course over the target, always a time of great danger. Over the target the bomb aimer gave the orders from his position lying prone in the nose of the aircraft. "Right, right, left, straight, hold it steady" while all the time the flak was coming up. Then from the bomb aimer " bombs gone" and the aircraft gave a lurch as it was relieved from its heavy bomb load. Again from the bomb aimer "steady for photograph". A photograph was always taken after the bombs had been dropped to access accuracy and to prove we had been over the target. Then, after an interminable wait, the bomb aimer called "photograph taken skipper" and we set course on the long journey home, a course which took us close to the search light belt between Karlsruhe and Mannheim, another dangerous place to be if a navigator made an error and an aircraft flew over it instead of round it. After a long and dangerous trip we landed back at base unharmed. It had been a baptism of fire and we had survived, although two of our Squadron crews did not.

In the circumstances it is remarkable that a considerable number of bombs fell in the target area and damage was done to all five ball bearing factories. But these results were obtained at a heavy cost, twenty three aircraft lost out of two hundred and twenty six despatched. That is 10 per cent. This included sixteen sent from 44 Squadron out of which two failed to return, just over 10 per cent.

It was on this raid that Sgt Jackson received a VC. He was the flight engineer of a Lancaster which was attacked and hit by a night fighter as they were leaving the target. A fire started in one of the petrol tanks in the starboard wing and armed with a fire extinguisher he climbed out on to the wing to put out the fire. He got badly burned and his parachute was damaged before he was swept away. His parachute was seen to be partly inflated and burning as he descended. The fire continued out of control and the pilot gave the order to the rest of the crew to bale out. Sgt Jackson, unable to control his descent, landed heavily with a broken ankle, one eye closed through burns, and his hands useless. He crawled to the nearest village where he was taken prisoner.

Two nights later we went to Oslo where we bombed and severely damaged an aircraft works. It was a long trip over the North Sea but there were no fighters or flak either en route or on the way back, and consequently none of our aircraft were lost. It was a lovely flight on the way back looking down from about seven thousand feet on fjords in the moonlight, with the moon shining on the dark calm sea below us. On 1 May we went to Toulouse to bomb a munitions factory and on return we were given a much welcome 9 days leave.

We were lucky to go on leave because on 3 May 5 Group, of which we were part, were ordered to bomb the large military depot and tank park at Mailly-le-Camp in Northern France. The target was of great importance for the coming battle of Normandy. It was believed to hold between 15,000 and 20,000 German troops and also to be the headquarters of the 21st Panzer Division. It was one of the principal German tank training centres in France. It went disastrously wrong. The marking of the first aiming point by Wing Commander Cheshire and Squadron Leader Shannon went entirely according to plan, but when the time came for two more Mosquitoes of No 617 Squadron to mark the second aiming point it was anticipated that there would be some difficulty, as by then this part of the target would be largely obscured by smoke. There was some delay which was very dangerous as the attack was being carried out in bright moonlight. But eventually the second aiming point was also accurately marked and a concentrated attack made. No other attacks were being made by Bomber Command that night and as a result the enemy was able to concentrate all the fighter squadrons allocated for the defence of northern France on Mailly, and in weather ideal for his purpose. Out of 338 aircraft despatched 45 were lost. The results may have justified these casualties as hundreds of buildings in the area were obliterated and the whole area of the camp was pitted with bomb craters. The report of the officer commanding 21st Panzer Division was afterwards captured and in a remarkable tribute to the effectiveness of the attack he said the main concentration was accurately aimed at the most important permanent buildings. In that part of the camp which was destroyed the concentration of bombs was so great that not only did the splinter proof trenches receive direct hits but even the bombs which missed choked them and caused them to cave in. Casualties among these highly trained German troops, a great number of whom had taken refuge in the trenches, was severe.

BACK TO WORK

Chapter three

Returning from leave we were back at work on the night of 19 May to take part in the bombing of Amiens. Out of 16 aircraft sent from 44 Squadron one failed to return. Two nights later on 21 May we were off to Kiel Bay to drop mines referred to as "Gardening" operations. We encountered flak all the way from the enemy coast to the target, but none of our aircraft went missing.

On the following night, 22 May, we went to Brunswick. Originally no more than a large market town, it had recently become an important industrial centre for light engineering and aircraft components. The town had been attacked several times before but with very little success. Earlier attacks failed because of bad weather, and also because it was believed that the enemy had been using dummy markers there, a device which there was every reasons to believe would be ineffective if No 5 Groups new tactics were used. This attack by two hundred and thirty five aircraft of No 5 Group was a failure due to the weather conditions being entirely different from that which had been forecast. Crews found unbroken cloud, very thick and low all the way from the coast to the target. Flares were dropped away from the target area, and without light it proved almost impossible to identify the aiming point. There was also considerable interference with the VHF radiotelephone system. There was fighter activity along the route and fourteen aircraft were lost, although happily none from 44 Squadron.

Following the Brunswick raid the decision was taken by Bomber Command to divert 5 Group from strategic bombing of industrial targets in Germany to tactical bombing of gun sites and troop concentrations in Northern France in support of the coming invasion. As a result Squadrons were liable to be called on at short notice and also operations for which we had been briefed could be cancelled at short notice causing great anti climax and frustration among crews. As a consequence we found ourselves bombing targets in Northern France.

On 27 May we attacked a gun site at Cherbourg and bombed from 5,500 feet. All aircraft returned safely. On 31 May we were sent to Maisy but all aircraft were recalled within a few miles of the French coast due to bad weather obscuring the aiming point. We jettisoned our bomb load 7 miles from the French coast. However two aircraft from our Squadron crashed attempting to land with a full bomb load, and although both aircraft were burnt out their crews escaped without injuries. On 2 June we went to attack a gun site at Wimereaux, a small town on the coast of France near Boulogne, but again owing to weather conditions we were recalled without bombing. In the case of the French targets it was the policy not to bomb unless the target could be identified in order to avoid killing civilians.

On 5 June we were despatched to bomb a gun site at Le Pernelle to round off the long series of pre-invasion softening up blows at the enemy's coastal defences. This was the eve of "D" day and as we flew back over the channel as dawn was breaking I had a magnificent view of the start of "D" day from about 6,000ft. The Skipper called the wireless operator and the navigator who could not see out from their positions in the aircraft, to the front, to come and see an "historic sight".

An historic sight it was; the skipper was quite right. Looking back over the years I have come to realise how fortunate I was to have seen such an important event in history unfolding before my eyes from such an advantageous position in the second pilot's seat. I looked down and stretching as far as the eye could see there was a succession of boats of every shape and size all going in one direction. The water behind them was streaked by the zig zag wakes of the ships taking evasive action as they reached the danger zone. Flak was bursting and there were gun flashes from several points along the French coast. I looked up to the sky. Not a German fighter to be seen, but hundreds of Allied aircraft, like the boats, all going in one direction, except the Lancasters, like ourselves, homeward bound. There were American and British fighters in great numbers and a large formation of American Flying Fortresses passed overhead, a thousand feet or so above us. Then soon after 7am we were back at our base in Lincolnshire.

The following night 6 June we attacked Caen to give tactical support to the Allied Forces who were trying to get a foothold on French soil. 44 Squadron lost one aircraft. On 8 June we went to Pontaubault to give the armies tactical support by attacking a railway junction. On 9 June to Etampes to attack another railway junction. Again we lost another aircraft from our Squadron. On 12 June we returned to Caen in tactical support of the Allied armies. We bombed from 6,000ft in 10/10 cloud. Following this trip we went on leave.

Lucky again for us because on the night of 21 June the Squadron, in our absence, took part in a raid to bomb oil storage plants at Wesseling in the Ruhr, a diversion from tactical bombing. It was a disaster. Out of 16 aircraft despatched from 44 Squadron 6 were lost, over a third. The force as a whole lost 37 aircraft. This was due to the unusual success of enemy night fighters because visibility above cloud on this the shortest night of the year was extraordinary good. By a great stroke of luck I had missed Nuremburg, Mailly-le-Camp and Wesseling. For had I been on any of those raids I have no doubt that I would not be writing these lines now.

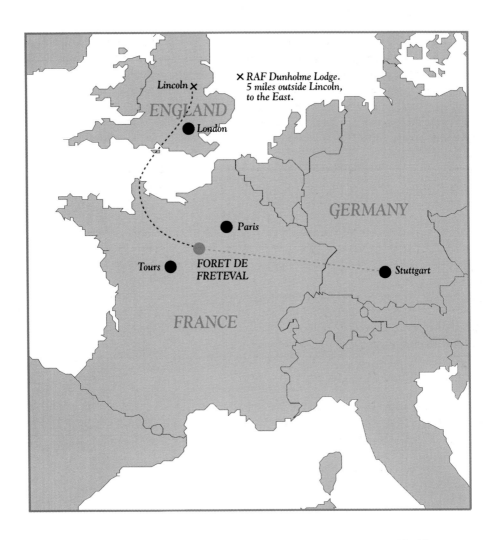

Lincoln ✕
✕ RAF Dunholme Lodge.
5 miles outside Lincoln,
to the East.

ENGLAND

● London

GERMANY

● Paris

Tours ●   FORET DE
            FRETEVAL

● Stuttgart

FRANCE

- - - - - - - - Approx track out on 18th July, after "D" day. If this raid had been
before "D" day the route would have been more direct. By flying over
the Cherburge peninsular there was more time in the air over Allied
held France.

- - - - - - - - Intended course to target.

THE LAST TRIP

(A single ticket only)

Chapter Four

On returning from leave the Squadron returned to tactical bombing. On 24 June we went to Pommerval to destroy a flying bomb site where we lost 2 out of the 15 aircraft despatched. On 27 June we bombed another flying bomb site, this time at Marquise where we lost one of our aircraft. On 4 July we were sent to another flying bomb site but returned before reaching the target because of engine failure. On 7 July we were despatched to St Leu d'Esserent to bomb underground caves in which flying bombs were stored. These caves had been excavated a number of years previously in the limestone hill overlooking the River Oise at St Leu. These caves had originally been used for mushroom growing by the French, and as far as could be ascertained their roof was about 25 feet thick. Some 15 feet of this was rather soft limestone, with a layer of soft clay above it. Photographs of the area showed that the depot was well protected by many anti aircraft gun sites. Although the ground defences we not as active as had been expected from the reconnaissance photographs of the site never the less we had to contend with determined air defence by night fighters and there were many losses, of which we lost 3 aircraft out of the eighteen sent from 44 Squadron. On 12 July we went to bomb railway yards at Culmont-Chalindrey and bombed from 5,000 feet. One of our aircraft failed to return.

It was over this target that I had the traumatic experience of hearing and seeing a man go to his doom. We had arrived at the target. The markers, that is the target indicators (TI's) had gone down but had been blown off target due to a strong wind. The controller gave the order over the RT for the main force to orbit the target while fresh target indicators of a different colour were dropped. Markers or target indicators were always dropped by a Pathfinder Mosquito flying in low over the target. The controller then had to fly in again low over the target to assess the accuracy. Meanwhile the main force had to orbit the target, not a pleasant experience, in this case at a height of only 5,000 feet. The Mosquito then made a second run over the target to assess the accuracy. As he did so flak came up, hit the Mosquito which burst into flames, and ploughed into the ground. Just before it did so the pilot called over the RT "take over number two they've got me." These were his last words. Next we heard over the RT "number two taking over going in to assess the marker" and then "marker OK main force go in and bomb". We went in and bombed and made for home. Marking the target was

29

a dangerous job and for this reason there were always two or three Mosquitoes standing by to take over if the first was hit.

On 14 July we attacked more railway yards at Villeneuve St George, an important railway centre South West of Paris where we bombed from 4,500feet. Happily all 44 Squadron aircraft returned from this trip. On 15 July, my 20th birthday, we were sent "Gardening" which was to drop mines in the Kattergat off Denmark. We lost one aircraft from 44 Squadron.

On 18 July we made a daylight trip to Caen. It was unusual for Lancasters to be used for daylight operations. We bombed from 6,000 feet the fortified German positions facing the Allied push towards Caen. We lost one aircraft from our Squadron. On 19 July we attacked a supply depot near Senlis from which all returned.

On 24 July we returned to Germany to bomb Stuttgart, an important industrial target in the Ruhr. We bombed from 20,000 feet. German night fighters were very active on this trip and 23 aircraft went missing although none from our Squadron. The next day aerial photographs showed that the raid had not been a success, most of the bombs having fallen short of the target. Consequently we were ordered to return to Stuttgart the following night, 25 July. This was to be our twenty fifth trip. It was our Skippers twenty sixth as all pilots did a trip first as "second dickie" with an experienced crew before taking their own crew on operations. We were therefore close to completing our first tour of thirty operations. It was not to be. We were one of three from 44 Squadron who failed to return.

Early in the evening of that day we joined the other crews on the Squadron to attend briefing, and were given our target for the night and the route to take. The weather forecast was good. After briefing we went to the crew room to collect our flying kit, parachute, emergency rations and escape pack. Then we climbed aboard the station transport and were taken to the dispersal point on the far side of the airfield, where our aircraft "E" for "Easy" was parked. The pilot and I did our pre flight checks, the two air gunners checked their guns, the navigator checked his charts, the radio operator his radio and radar equipment and the bomb aimer his bombsight. The pilot and I started the four Rolls Royce engines, which sprang into life with a tremendous roar, and then, when it was our turn, we taxied out to the take off point where we awaited our turn to depart. Other aircraft were in front of us and others behind. When our turn came we turned on to the runway. The aircraft ahead of us was just airborne.

The green light flashed from the control caravan, the pilot called for full power and we rolled down the runway gaining speed, and then slowly, because we had a full fuel and bomb load, we staggered into the air.

We headed north from Lincoln to gain height. It took time to climb with a full bomb load, and we then turned towards the Channel and Caen. We had to reach full height, about 14,000 feet, before reaching enemy territory, in the area around Caen. As we flew over enemy territory anti-aircraft flak came up at us, a frightening sight, particularly when out of the darkness another aircraft is hit by it, and bursts it into flames, plunging to the ground in ball of fire. With 2,000 gallons of petrol on board the glow lights up the whole sky for miles around, putting other aircraft into danger, by exposing us all. Further away we saw an exchange of tracer bullets. An aircraft was being attacked by German fighters. It burst into flames and fell to the ground. Then things quietened down and we flew on in the darkness, because the main anti-aircraft defences and German fighters were concentrated immediately inside Germany.

Just as we thought we were going to have a quiet time until we reached Germany we suddenly felt a large thump from the rear of the aircraft which immediately went into a steep dive. The pilot pulled hard on the control column and called me to help, but in spite of us both pulling on it, it made no difference. The aircraft continued to dive. We were never quite sure whether we had been hit in the rear by anti-aircraft fire or a German fighter, or whether an aircraft above us, of which there were many out that night, had got into difficulties and jettisoned its bombs, one of which had landed on our tail and sent us out of control.

It was immediately clear the aircraft was out of control. The skipper, that is the captain and pilot, gave us the dreaded order: "bale out". I put on my parachute, snatched off my helmet which was combined with my head set, and went down into the nose of the aircraft. We always wore our helmets and headsets from the moment of starting the engines. They muffled the thundering sound of the four Rolls Royce engines. Now, with my helmet off, the noise from the engines combined with the rush of air through the aircraft when the bomb aimer opened the hatch and dived, out was deafening. My turn next and I hesitated. A thought flashed through my mind. Had the order to bale out been rescinded and I had not heard it? The fear of loneliness gripped me. While flying the crew were constantly in communication with each other through the intercom. Now, without my headset, I was all alone and could not hear a thing above the roar of the engines and the rush of wind tearing through the aircraft. It had happened on one occasion that a pilot had given the order to bale out and then managed to get control of the aircraft, and flew it back to base with half his crew, the other half having by then baled out. Was this to be my fate?

"Bloody hell", I said to myself "this cannot be happening to me, think quickly for God's sake."

I felt sweat seeping out of me. I could feel beads of water oozing from my forehead. I was experiencing real fear, stark undiluted fear. I felt stricken, incapable of movement or clear thought. My immediate reaction was that things must take their course. A voice of reason then came into my mind. "For God's sake there is going to be a crash, I am about to die, so this is what it feels like."

I pictured what would happen when the aircraft hit the ground. A blinding flash and the noise of tearing tortured metal. "Oh God what a waste my education has been. My parents will be heartbroken. What a fool I have been. I should not have volunteered. I do not know what is happening, except that I am in the process of crashing and dying. Why did I not enjoy life more while I had it? Please God get this over with and quickly".

Then Ted, the navigator, came up behind me and yelled "get a F***ing move on". He gave me a push, and out I went into space at about 10,000 feet. He made my mind up for me and thereby saved my life.

DANGEROUS JOURNEY

(The long road home)

Chapter Five

What did it feel like to fall into space on a dark night at 10,000 feet? A good description of how it feels can be found in that lovely children's book *Alice in Wonderland*. Alice describes running after the white rabbit as follows:-

> *"Alice ran across the field after it (the white rabbit) and was just in time to see it pop down a large rabbit hole under the hedge. In another moment Alice we nt down after it, never once considering how in the world she was to get out again. Alice had not a moment to think about stopping herself before she found herself falling down a very deep well. Either the well was very deep or she fell very slowly, for she had plenty of time as she went down to look about her, and to wonder what was going to happen next. She tried to look down and make out what she was coming to, but it was too dark to see anything. Well, thought Alice to herself, after such a fall as this I shall think nothing of tumbling down the stairs! How brave they'll all think me at home! Down, down, down. Would the fall never come to an end? I wonder how many miles I've fallen by this time? Then she said aloud "I must be getting near the centre of the earth"! Down, down, down. There was nothing else to do so Alice began talking to herself again, when suddenly thump! Thump! Down she came on a heap of dry leaves, and the fall was over. Alice was not a bit hurt and she jumped up on to her feet in a moment. She looked up but it was all dark overhead. There was not a moment to be lost. Away went Alice like the wind."*

My feelings were much the same as Alice.

Like Alice I felt the cold rush of night air. As I somersaulted into space I pulled the parachute handle before I had counted the regulation number of ten. Nothing happened, and then just as I began to think it was not going to work I was pulled up with a comforting jerk. The parachute had opened and I began to descend slowly to earth. It was like Alice falling down a very deep well. At that moment I experienced a sense of relief. I was alive and my parachute was lowering me to earth. My descent probably only lasted about three minutes, but during the time I was in mid air with nothing but space under the soles of my shoes, for thousands of feet, it seemed much longer. It was a dark night and like Alice I could see nothing above me and nothing below me. I had plenty of time to think as I went down, to look about me, and to wonder what was going to happen next. Then there was a sudden vivid flash followed by an explosion and for a second the whole sky was lit up like a photoflash. It was our aircraft which had crashed into the ground with a full bomb load. If anyone had still been in it they would have been blown to pieces. After the explosion the darkness closed in again like velvet, and all was quiet. Down, down, down. Would the fall never come to an end. As there was nothing else to do I began talking to myself. Then, after two or three minutes, I saw the ground below me approaching fast. Seconds later thump! Thump! I hit the ground heavily and found myself in a field, shaken and bruised but otherwise unharmed. I was very lucky. I hid my parachute, and like Alice, made off like the wind before anyone could come and find me. There was not a moment to lose.

It was essential to get moving immediately, for two good reasons. Firstly, if I had been seen landing, that would be the spot which would have been searched, and therefore the greater the distance from where I had landed the better the chance of not getting caught. Secondly, if you do nothing in such circumstances shock can take over and you make no attempt to escape. Activity was considered the best way to overcome shock. I therefore ran as hard as I could, and for as long as I could, to put as much distance between myself and the place where I had landed as possible, before anyone came to look for me. When I could run no more I continued at walking pace.

I kept off the roads because there was a curfew after dark, and any one seen out was liable to be shot. I therefore made my way across fields. On one occasion I was crossing a field and when I got to the middle of it I saw what looked like tracer bullets falling near me. At first I thought it was my imagination, but taking no chances I ran to the hedge at the side of the field and hid, and the shooting stopped. I tried again and the same thing happened. When I got into the middle of the field the shooting began again. After several attempts with the same thing happening I took a different route. What it was I do not know. I can only think it was the Resistance, some distance away, who since there was a curfew at night thought that I must have been a German, and decided to take a shot at me.

At this juncture I began to feel very depressed and lonely with no one to talk to. I had no idea where I was, and no idea when I would meet anybody. Indeed, who I would meet or when. I had no food and no idea when or where I would get any, apart from what was in my escape pack. The escape kits with which we were issued before take off consisted of a plastic container, the contents of which consisted of such items as chocolate, Horlicks tablets, a tiny compass, matches, energy tablets, and even a small sewing kit. We were also given a waterproof packet containing maps and money of the country over which we were flying. I had nowhere to sleep and I did not know where I was, except that I was about 45 minutes flying time into German Occupied France. It was intensely lonely on my own in a foreign land. I did not know what had happened to the rest of the crew, whether or not they had all managed to bale out. I spent the night wandering about the French countryside. It was the first time I had been outside England.

It is a rude awakening and a daunting experience to find yourself in a situation such as this. You are all alone and everything you have been accustomed to take for granted no longer exists. Your plight suddenly looms large. About midnight I came to a little village with a small church in the centre. It was unlocked. I pushed the door open, went inside, and sat down to collect my thoughts. Then, after about 20 minutes or so, I left.

In these circumstances you realise that the every day little things which you never normally think about are not available. I was thirsty. What about a drink of water? What about something to eat? What about somewhere to sleep, or someone to talk to? I had no one to grumble to except myself, and what is worse I had no idea when I was going to be able to get these
simple requirements, if at all. And what about status? You have none. You have nothing. You are just alive. A millionaire's son has no more status than the son of a beggar, and no better chance of surviving. I decided that as the Allied armies were in the Caen area I would try to walk there. It seemed to be the best option. I reckoned it would be a distance of no more than 200 miles north-west from where I was.

FIRST LIGHT

Chapter Six

When dawn broke I hid under a hedge and slept all morning. I awoke about mid-day and heard voices coming from the field but remained hidden as I did not want to be seen. I did not know what those people would do if they found me. Not all French people, even at this stage of the war, were pro British, and there were many inducements and incentives to betray an allied airman. Whereas, on the contrary, to be found giving help to an airman almost certainly resulted in death or the concentration camp. I felt very lonely and the situation I was in came home to me. I could not imagine what was in store for me, what would I be doing the next day or even later that day, what was I going to do about food, who would I meet next. These were matters which I had never before had to consider or bother about.

At this point my morale was at it's lowest. As I had decided to remain hidden under the hedge until dusk there was nothing to occupy my mind except the enormity of the task before me. Also I knew that it would be about the time when my parents would be receiving the dreaded telegram to say I was missing. They would think the worst. If only I could tell them I was alive and unharmed. It was the sense of the agony I was inflicting on them rather than myself that made me feel so bad, even guilty. My sense of isolation became vivid and intense and I could do nothing about it.

In the early evening about an hour before sunset I got up from the hedge and on to the road, to take advantage of the daylight to see where I was before it got dark. I passed some people and to my relief they took no notice of me. I had no disguise except that over the top part of my RAF battle dress I was wearing a brown linen jacket. With my penknife I had cut off the leg part of my black flying boots around the ankle, which transformed them into what looked like an ordinary pair of shoes. I came to a village called Langey. It was a tiny village with a little church in the centre, and I walked through it. There were people about but they took no notice of me. I walked beyond the village and then, feeling sick and tired, I crept into a haystack and fell asleep.

I awoke in the morning as dawn was breaking, feeling cold but better. Having passed people the previous evening who did not appear to regard me as unusual I considered that my disguise, such as it was, blended well into the surroundings - or at least I did not stick out like as sore thumb! So I decided not to waste time hiding by day and walking at night but instead to proceed on my way in daylight. It would be quicker and easier than by night.

I was also encouraged by the fact that there were signposts at cross roads, and place names, which I could identify on my map. This was a great help in locating my position. Back in 1940 when Britain was under threat of a German invasion all signposts were taken down in order to avoid helping the invaders. The Germans did not do this in the occupied countries which was of considerable help, to evaders like myself.

I left the haystack as dawn was breaking, and soon approached another village. All was quiet until I approached the cross roads in the centre, when I heard the sound of heavy vehicles approaching, which sent my heart down to my feet. It was not good news. I was fortunate. A few yards away there was an open gate which lead into a walled garden. I leaped into it and hid behind a bush, just in time because four or five German lorries full of troops passed by where I had stood only a few seconds before. When they had gone I continued on my way through the village, and into the open countryside beyond, and soon heard the very same sound of heavy vehicles again. There were no hedges at the side of the road at this point, and so I ran at great speed across a field and hid behind a farm building. Peering round it, I saw the same or similar lorries pass along the road again, in the opposite direction. Seconds only had saved me from being discovered. This time their were no soldiers on board. Just the drivers and a soldier with a machine gun on the running board. I survived to continue my journey.

When the road was clear I continued on my way and headed towards Normandy. I passed people during the day. They paid no attention to me, which gave me confidence to continue. It was lucky for me that it was summer and warm and dry. As I walked I passed local people going about their daily tasks. Consequently I felt less exposed and, since they took no notice of me, I felt that my makeshift disguise was proving satisfactory and that I was blending into the surroundings, and that I might make it. After another days walk I spent another night under a hedge and then continued on my way. As I had completed only a very small part of the 200 miles or so needed to reach Allied lines I became very pessimistic about reaching my destination. Nevertheless I continued. There was no alternative.

Later that morning I had another frightening experience. While continuing my walk along a narrow road I could see a T junction about 1/4 of a mile ahead, when, to my horror, up to the T junction came a German army car with four soldiers in it. I thought my luck had run out. There was just a chance that if it turned left at the junction and went in the opposite direction I would be all right. It did not. It turned right and came towards me. I thought this is it. The war is over for me now. I shall be shot or at best spend the rest of the war in a prisoner of war camp. I walked with my head down. The car was travelling very slowly as it approached me, then passed me, so close I could have touched it. But to my utter surprise and relief it passed me without stopping and continued on its way and I continued on mine. Unlike

Lot's wife, I did not dare turn round to have a look. When I did pluck up enough courage to twist round and look it was nowhere to be seen. I could not believe my luck, and concluded that my disguise was even good enough to fool the Germans.

MY JOURNEY CONTINUES

Chapter Seven

Later that day, while continuing my walk, I was again lucky in a different way. I foolishly gave myself away. As I walked I was chewing some chewing gum, something I should not have been doing, because neither chewing gum nor sweets were available in France, at that time. Chewing gum, therefore, was a give away and I should have known better, but by this time I was very tired and getting careless. However, I was lucky because it worked in my favour. A boy on a bicycle passed me and noticed this, and stopped and called to me. There was no one else in sight at the time. I walked over to him and he asked "Are you RAF?" Yes, I said. "Then follow me". He led me off the road on to a track and told me to lie under the hedge, while he went for help.

What should I do? Should I wait in the hope that the youth was a genuine helper, or was he going to inform the Germans? Would it be better to move off while I still had my freedom, in the hope that I would not be found? After all, not all the locals were friendly. It was a great temptation to hand an airman over to the German authorities because it would be awarded with privileges such as extra food, money and freedom from harassment. Whereas to be caught helping an airman, even to the extent of only giving him something to eat, meant torture, death or the concentration camp. After much mental deliberation I decided to stay.

About half an hour later a car drove up the track with the same youth in the passenger seat. The driver got out. He was a tall man who spoke good English and I felt from the start that I could trust him, and that in deciding to stay I had made the right decision. He gave me a civilian overcoat to put on and told me to get in the back of the car, and we drove off.

It was wonderful to be riding in a car after nearly three days of walking alone along French roads. He told me he was the local Doctor and that his wife was English. She came from Bournemouth and they had married there just before the war. We passed through a village and the boy got out. I thanked him and said good bye and I continued the journey with the Doctor. We came to a farm. The Doctor took me into the kitchen and introduced me to the farmer and his wife. After a conversation the Doctor left. I never saw the boy or the Doctor again. We were told never to keep the name or address of helpers, so that if we were subsequently caught we could not give them away.

The farmers wife began to cook an omelette. I was very hungry having had nothing to eat except a few bars of chocolate and some sweets, which I had on me, and the rations from my emergency escape kit. We were always

41

issued with a bar of milk chocolate and some boiled sweets, before take off, to sustain us on our flight. Our emergency pack contained a plastic bag and some purifying tablets so that we could get water from a stream to drink, but I had not wanted to risk it, and had only used it to rinse my mouth. Consequently I was thirsty as well as hungry. I asked for, and was given, a glass of water from a bucket of water which had been boiled. The tap water did not seem to be used for drinking. I was so dehydrated that once given a glass of water I could not stop drinking until I had consumed a vast quantity. By the time I had quenched my thirst the omelette was ready and with a quantity of French bread I enjoyed a much needed meal.

When I had eaten I was taken into a room where two men were asleep in a double bed. My host woke them up and to my surprise and delight one was Ken the wireless operator from our crew and the other a Canadian air gunner who had been shot down a few days earlier. It was a great comfort to be with friends. I was given a bed to myself in a separate room. I was very tired and slept until midday the following day. When I awoke I was told that my two friends were already up and so I joined them. We were told to stay in the house and to keep away from windows as there were Germans in the district who would call and ask questions if they saw anything unusual.

That evening we sat down to a meal with the farmer and his wife, and some of their friends. We had a good meal, with several courses, consisting mainly of vegetables. As soon as we sat down the farmer produced a bottle of Champagne, something I had never had before. It was soon consumed, but he produced another one, and when that was empty yet another one! This went on throughout the meal and into the evening. He told us that a few weeks earlier a train with a large quantity of Champagne was passing nearby on its way to the Head Quarters of the Germany Army, which was moving into Normandy to cover for the Allied invasion. As the train was passing through that part of France it was bombed by the RAF and from the wreckage local farmers extracted a large quantity for themselves, before the Germans got to it, and so our host said he was delighted to be able to celebrate with us. I remember thinking to myself what an extraordinary situation it was that, having gone through all I had in the past three days, to finish up with a Champagne supper inside enemy territory. We went to bed that night suffering from the effects of too much Champagne.

The next morning we went into the kitchen for breakfast and found there two men in civilian clothes whom we imagined were French locals. It turned out that they were both RAF. One, Peter Berry, was English. The other, Pierre, a Belgian fighter pilot who had joined the RAF after Dunkirk. Both had been shot down some weeks earlier. The Belgian could speak fluent French, which was to be a great asset. After breakfast our uniforms were taken from us and we were given civilian clothes, albeit threadbare and ill fitting. We were told we were going on a long walk but we were not told our destination. We then set off with the two newcomers leading and we were joined by the farmers wife and some children and friends, one of whom had a bicycle. On the way we were joined by a few more airmen who had been brought to join us by another Frenchman. By mid afternoon footsore and weary we approached a large forest covered in thick foliage. At this point we said goodbye to our French friends and thanked them for looking after us and they turned round and went home. We then followed Berry and Pierre into the forest.

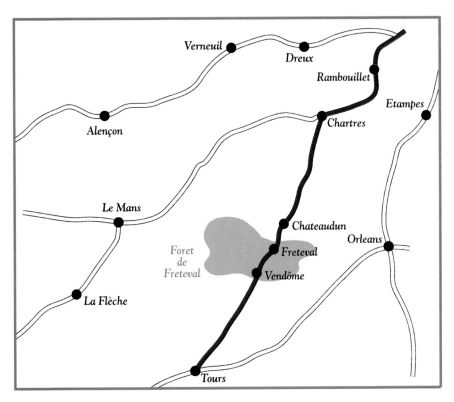

MAP SHOWING THE SITE OF
THE "CAMP" FOR AIRMEN IN
THE FORET DE FRETEVAL 1944

THE SECRET FOREST

Chapter Eight

Deep in the heart of Northern France, in the area between Chateaudun and Vendome, and close to the little town of Cloyes, lies a very large forest. It is over 20 miles long and 10 miles wide. It is the Forest of Freteval. Thick, dark and uninviting, and surrounded by flat open fields, it provided an ideal venue for clandestine activities, including parachute operations.

Once inside the forest we discovered we were not alone. There were over 70 scruffy and unshaven weary looking men wearing ill fitting clothes, the whole looking like an army of tramps. They were Allied airmen who had been brought to the forest and hidden there by the Resistance, over the previous weeks, from in fact May. To our great delight we met our pilot. This meant that Ken and I did not have to undergo an interrogation to ensure that we were genuine escapers, and not Nazi infiltrators. The Resistance lost a lot through Germans impersonating shot down airmen. During the next two days our bomb aimer was brought in, and also our navigator.

Hitherto the main line of escape for airmen shot down over the Continent, if fortunate enough to have contacted the Resistance, was by a number of organised escape lines extending across Belgium, Holland and France down to the Pyrenees. From here an experienced mountain guide would lead them at night over the mountains into neutral Spain, and then they were taken to Gibraltar. From there they would be returned to the UK. Thus an airmen shot down, over say Belgium, would be hidden in a safe house by the Resistance, given civilian clothes and a false identity card, and passed from one guide to another until eventually reaching St Jean de Luze, they were then hidden until a group of airmen had been collected and then they were all taken over the Pyrenees. Such a journey could take up to six months or longer.

As D day approached it was realised both by British Intelligence and the Resistance that these escape lines would not be able to function any longer, because the Germans would be moving large numbers of troops into Northern France, with the result that all roads and railway stations would be heavily guarded, making the exercise too risky if not impossible. An alternative plan had to be devised. It would have been too dangerous to leave airmen for long in safe houses, and furthermore with bombing operations being stepped up around D-day and an increasing number of airmen having to bale out, it would be impossible to find enough safe accommodation.

47

As a result of discussions between MI9 (the section of British Intelligence dealing with escapes) and the Resistance, the idea was formed of finding a large wood in which airmen could be hidden "under the noses of the Germans". Hopefully without being discovered. The idea was conceived in London at MI9 between Airey Neave and Baron Jean de Blommaert, a Belgian who had been heavily involved in the Resistance and who had escaped to England in order to avoid arrest by the Gestapo, who were on his trail.

Taking a map of the region of Chartres - Chateaudun - Orleans they selected the extensive and thickly wooded area between Chateaudun and Vendome known as the Forest of Feteval, near the small town of Cloyes. Surrounding it were many open spaces suitable for parachute operations. Everyone concerned was sure that by setting up the camp in the forest they would improve the airmen's chance of safety. Still more important it would lessen the risk to the helpers and their families who would otherwise have to shelter airmen in their homes. It was foreseen that retreating Germans might have ragged nerves, Oradour-sur-Glane having provided tragic evidence that this assumption was correct. [1]

MI9 was haunted by the thought of airmen caught at large in occupied territory being massacred by retreating German troops. Therefore it was decided to proceed with the plan code named " Sherwood" after Robin Hood and Nottingham Forest.

In April 1944 de Blommaert was parachuted back into France to organise the operation. It was also decided to send Squadron Leader Lucien Boussa, also a Belgian and a trained pilot, who had escaped after Dunkirk and joined the RAF and had fought in the Battle of Britain. He was accompanied by a radio operator to assist him once the camp had been made ready. De Blommaert had already made visits to the Forest of Freteval and he decided to set up his headquarters near Cloyes. As he had foreseen he found that there were farmers bakers and other tradesmen who were willing to supply food for us on the black market. Blommaert also reached an agreement with the Resistance that there would be no acts of sabotage or other subversive activity against the Germans in or near the Forest de Freteval. It was hoped the German army would eventually be forced to retreat towards the Seine,

---

[1] Just after D Day an SS Panzer Division was on its way north from the south to reinforce the defence of the Normandy landing beaches. The Division's progress was delayed by the French Resistance, who cut down trees along its route, and who also subjected it to incessant sniping. Near Limoges it was held up for 48 hours. This delay, which was significant, helped the Allies to secure a foothold on the beaches. The Germans took reprisals.
The SS entered the small village of Oradour-sur-Glane, about 25 miles from Limoges, and raised it to the ground. The men were all gathered together and murdered by machine gun fire. The Germans herded the women and children into the village church and then set it alight. All inside were burnt alive.
The village has been left as it was and can be visited today as a reminder of the horrors of war.

leaving the forest in a no-mans-land between Le Mans and Chateaudun. This is in fact what happened and the camp was liberated in late August 1944 after some of the airmen had been hidden in the thick forest foliage for over three months.

On 13 May Boussa with his wireless operator arrived at the forest having travelled overland from Spain, along the escape line in reverse, with orders to proceed with the plan. Boussa was nearly forty, spare and energetic. He had been chosen to maintain discipline and morale. To keep a large number of airmen of different nationalities secretly hidden in a forest deep inside enemy territory for up to three months was a difficult assignment. As he was a serving RAF Officer of senior rank who had distinguished himself in air combat he was able to enforce the rules in the camp. He was given instructions on security and on the interrogation of airmen on their arrival at the camp. He spoke English well.

The success of the Sherwood plan depended on the personal leadership of Boussa and Blommaert. Their principle problem was to keep order in the forest and to prevent the men, through impatience, from making attempts to escape on their own and getting caught. They were helped by the high quality of the local Resistance who were based on Chateaudun. One of the leaders was Omer Jubault, a gendarme from Cloyes. He was shrewd and devoted and had already risked arrest for his help to the Resistance and had now disappeared from the police force. Taking two foresters into his confidence he selected a site among the trees well concealed from the Cloyes - Vendome road along which German military transport was passing at all hours. The proposed location was deemed suitable, the trees and foliage, being thick, would hide all activity. A spring of pure water was discovered just at the edge of the forest and the slight slope leading into the wood provided easy surveillance of the approach of any suspicious person.

For those who did not experience it, it is difficult to imagine life under German occupation at this period of the war. Rationing was extremely strict and there was virtually no coffee, rice or chocolate, except on the black market. There was practically no fuel or petrol. Nonetheless local farmers were able to supply the camp with small quantities of meat, butter and eggs, and importantly, bread. Two airmen were selected as cooks and cooked on charcoal fires which gave little smoke. On the night of 6/7 July a supply operation took place. Containers were dropped containing tents, food and essential medicines. But by the time I arrived in the forest there were not enough tents for all of us and some of us had to sleep under cover of parachutes, which had been salvaged.

Eden Camp, Malton
AGM, April 2000
The President of the RAF Escaping Society
Air Chief Marshal Sir Lewis Hodges
talking to the Hon Secretary,
Elizabeth Harrison

Escape lines
Memorial Weekend
May 2003
Andree Dumon
Code name *Nadine*, at Allandale, Leeds

Comete
October 1993
Frank Dell,
Chairman of the RAF Escaping Society
and **Andre de Jongh,**
who was known by her code name
of *Dedee*

Jean Francois Northomb
code name *Franco*.
He took over the Comete line after
Dedee was arrested

INSIDE THE FOREST OF HIDDEN MEN

Chapter Nine

On the 6th of June 1944 the first airmen who had hitherto been lodged in the homes of Resistance workers were brought to the forest and life in the woods began. From May onwards bombing operations over Northern France were increased and as more airmen were being shot down the camp grew in size and so, towards the end of June, it became necessary y to start a second camp. The first camp in which I was became Camp no 1. It was situated in the north part of the forest near the Bellande Farm.

The second camp was started on the 24 June and designated Camp no 2. It was located about ten kilometres to the south of Camp no1. Baron Jean de Blomaert, known to us as "Big John" as he was a tall blonde Belgian, took charge of Camp no 2 and actually lived in it. He had caused the Germans so much trouble and had worked under so many assumed names the Germans referred to him as the Fox. On 12 June he, together with Omer Jubault and others, had carried out a raid on a German ammunition centre and captured arms and ammunitionfor the benefit of the Resistance.

Lucien Boussa, who we called cousin Lucien, took charge of Camp no 1. Lucien, unlike Blomaert, did not live in the camp with us. Instead he made his headquarters in the local railway station, the manager of which was a French patriot, where the comings and goings of the travellers would hide his contacts with the underground. Boussa visited us daily bringing news of the outside world. In particular how the invasion was progressing, which was of particular concern to us. Guides were needed to lead airmen to the forest. Blomaert recruited a number of guides who had worked for the Comète Escape line to supplement those available in the locality. Among these was Virginia d'Lake and her husband, who had been the chief organiser in Paris.

Life in the forest was boring, rough and dangerous. Boredom and anxiety were extremely difficult to combat. We passed our time, thanks to fine weather, sunbathing and talking. It was extremely hot most of the time. Two airmen were selected as cooks and cooked on charcoal fires which gave off little smoke. There was a well of clear water on the edge of the forest from which we were able to draw water, but in view of the numbers
involved there was little enough for drinking and still less for washing. We had some razors and soap and other basics which we shared and so we were able to shave with cold water. With only a few bowls to put water in the amount of washing we could do was very limited and we got pretty filthy. Some even suffered from lice and itched continuously. The washing of

clothes was quite out of the question and we lived for weeks, and some lived for nearly three months, in the same clothes, night and day.

Such basics as we had came from an air drop which had taken place on the night of 6/7 July before I arrived in the forest. Fifteen containers were dropped containing tents, food, medicine and some clothing. Most air drops were intended for the Resistance and mainly consisted of weapons and ammunition, and the occasional spy for good measure. Air drops were dangerous business and many Resistance workers were arrested during them. A field would be selected and its location radioed to London. One night, a day or two before I arrived in the Forest, there had been a fight between the Resistance and German troops following an air drop which took place in the fields adjoining the forest. A number of Resistance were killed, but the Germans did not enter the forest and the camp lived on.

From logs and branches we made tables and chairs. A radio set had been brought into the forest and we were able to hear how the battle of Normandy was progressing. Any important announcements were posted to a tree which served as the camp notice board. We maintained a degree of discipline, rising between 6 and 7 when we had breakfast, which consisted of a mug of coffee and a slice of bread and butter. We then made up our beds of straw and camouflaged our tents and other items with branches in case they could be seen from the air. We also took turns to do sentry duty at points where we could see any suspicious persons approaching the forest. There was not much we could have done, except to warn the others, and every man would have had to run for it.

Fear and anxiety were ever present knowing that if the Germans had discovered us, and their vehicles frequently passed on the road beside the forest, we would have been shot without any questions being asked. Food was meagre. Lunch consisted of beans, sometimes a little meat was added, usually rabbit meat. Supper, like breakfast, consisted of a mug of coffee and a slice of bread and butter. The forest was full of wasps nests. They were buzzing around everywhere and swarmed on us the moment we began to eat. We were continually being stung. I was stung several times a day. On one day I was stung over a dozen times.

The small quantities of meat, vegetables, butter and bread were supplied by local farmers thanks to the contacts made by Pierre. A local miller organised the delivery of fresh bread brought by a young girl in a horse drawn cart. She made the journey through forest rides for several weeks, in spite of being machine gunned on one occasion by Allied aircraft in mistake for German transport. French patriots even risked the curfew to obtain fish for us from the River Loir.

At night after dark we had to keep very quite and speak in whispers because voices carry very easily on warm summers nights. Such food as we got had to be obtained locally. We were fortunate in having Pierre, the Belgian among us, who could speak fluent French, and he had acquired a bicycle. Thus he could contact local people for supplies and, if necessary, as it sometimes was, to pay for them.

Odd though it may seem we were not short of money as all of us had been issued with a quantity of francs in our escape kits, which most of us had not had to use. In any case Lucien on his daily visits always had plenty of money available should it be needed. It was strange to be in a situation where we had no possessions and barely enough food on which to exist but we had plenty of money which, in the circumstances, was of no use.

At the end of July the camp had grown to 100 including some wounded and sick. A male nurse among the airmen was appointed who looked after the sick and slightly wounded in a hospital tent. Severely wounded were hidden by an elderly French woman in her house on the edge of the forest which served as a hospital. They were treated in secret by a doctor from Cloyes and an American pilot had a successful operation to remove an appendix.

A few days after I had arrived in the forest with Ken, our radio operator, our navigator and then our bomb aimer were brought in and finally Frank, our rear gunner. He came in unusual circumstances. He arrived with a guide and was hobbling on a stick with one leg in plaster. Some days earlier while on his way to the forest with a guide they had decided to go into a field to rest. While resting the guide showed Frank an old revolver with which he was armed. Frank produced an efficient and up to date RAF revolver which he should not have had and began to show his guide how it worked. We were not allowed firearms and certainly not allowed to go on operations carrying firearms. However Frank had a very persuasive way with women and persuaded the WAAF sergeant in the armoury to let him have a revolver every time we went on operations, which was strictly against regulations. He hid it under his battledress and returned it after every operation. He felt he might have need of it one day. While demonstrating it to the French guide and forgetting the safety catch was not on the guide accidentally pulled the trigger and the bullet went through Frank's ankle. The hapless guide finding himself in this predicament managed to help Frank to a safe house where the Doctor from Cloyes attended to him and put his leg in plaster. A few days later Frank was able to resume his journey to the forest. This meant that six out of the seven members of the crew had been collected by the Resistance and brought to the forest. Only one of the crew, Tom, the other air gunner was killed and did not make it. The rest of us got back but the only one to receive a decoration was Frank who was awarded the DFC. He had been wounded in action but not in air combat.

Incredible as it may seem by the middle of August 1944 152 airmen were living and being fed and watered in the two camps hidden in the forest. It was necessary to have as few people as possible who knew of our existence. Blomeart arranged for agents to report to him any rumours and information of enemy troop movements. Sentries were posted at all times, especially at dawn, Through the day and night they were at the entrances to the forest. I spent a lot of time on sentry duty. It relieved the boredom of sitting among the trees all day, and it was interesting to observe the road that ran passed the forest. It was mostly farm traffic that passed but occasionally a German military vehicle would go bye. It gave me a peculiar sensation to see the enemy pass within a few yards of where I was hiding, but not realising that I or any of us were there. In the event of an alarm it would have to be every man for himself. Every man had his escape kit which contained emergency rations money and maps.

One day there was panic when a scruffy man approached the forest. The sentries brought him in and he was interrogated. He could not speak a word of English, nor of French nor of any language known to anyone in the forest. One or two thought they could detect a Russia dialect and produced the theory that he may have been a Russian deserter who had roamed into that part of France. We never did discover who he was as nobody could understand his language. We decided to call him Cogi for want of any other name. However we dare not let him go as he might have been picked up by the Germans, or unfriendly French, and led them to the forest. We therefore kept him prisoner and gave him the dirty and unpleasant jobs to do.

One day when I was on sentry duty Lucien came into the forest looking very worried. We all gathered around him. He brought bad news. Virginia had been arrested. (Virginia de Lake mentioned earlier). He told us that it was known she was under interrogation by the Gestapo and that if she gave anything away the Germans would be along immediately. He warned us to be on the alert and that we were in danger because he thought the Gestapo would get information out of her.

Virginia de Lake was an American lady who was working in Paris before the war where she had met her husband, Albert. When, in 1940, France collapsed they joined the Resistance in Paris and did a lot of work. In particular they provided accommodation in their flat for escaping Allied airmen passing through Paris en route to the Pyrenees and Spain. By the spring of 1944 Virginia had been warned by her friends that the Gestapo were on her trail and that she ought to leave Paris for her own safety. She did, and came to help in the Eure et Loir area where the camp was being established.

Her first assignment in this part of the country was to guide some airmen to the forest. She was to meet the airmen at Chateaudun railway station to where they were being brought by train. The airmen were then to proceed to the forest, one on foot walking and two on a hay cart. Virginia was to walk some distance ahead of the hay cart and lead them to the forest. She had not been to the forest before and so was given a sketch of the route on a small piece of paper. On the way a German patrol car stopped because the officer in it wanted to enquire the way to somewhere nearby, and he assumed she was a local and could help him. He did not suspect anything. Unfortunately for Virginia the German officer was very fluent in French and in the course of the conversation he detected that Virginia was speaking with an American accent. He became suspicious and took her in for questioning. Virginia was interrogated and tortured but never disclosed what she had been doing. She even managed to swallow the piece of paper with the route to the forest on it, and we airmen survived for another day.

For her bravery Virginia was sent to the notorious Ravensbruck concentration camp where she nearly died. She was a living skeleton when the Americans rescued her at the end of the war. I am pleased to say she fully recovered and was able to live a normal life. I have a photograph which I took of her in June 1967 looking fit and well.

The arrest of Virginia caused very great concern to the escorts and also to us in the forest. Sentries were reinforced and we were all tense and ready to flee at the least alert. Mons Hallouin, the forester who with his wife lived in a cottage a short distance from the edge of the forest, had a fire ready to light in their grate if the Germans were seen coming so that the smoke from the chimney would be a warning of approach.

Once in the middle of the night we heard the sound of heavy vehicles on the road outside the forest. It was a German convoy passing through. One of the vehicles broke down and it was moved off the road on to the track leading up to the forest. We could hear hammering and men's voices while it was being worked on. We all kept quiet and very still. Fortunately by morning everything had moved away and we lived yet another day. Also in July Maxime Plateau, who supplied much of the food for the forest, was arrested following a parachute drop of arms intended for Resistance groups in the area. Tortured and sent to a concentration camp he revealed nothing.

Towards the end as the Allies began to advance towards our area RAF bombers started bombing nearby woods in which the Germans had stored ammunition. Ironically we were in danger of being hit by our own bombs. We stood in fear watching the RAF, but fortunately they did not fly over the wood where we were.

It had been known to Blomaert that ammunition had been stored in the adjacent woods but he considered this fact an advantage because the Germans would be less likely to suspect the presence of allied airmen in the locality. Further, it would deter busy bodies and nosey parkers from prowling round and telling everybody what they had seen. However it was very frightening, seeing neighbouring woods being bombed, and wondering if ours would in turn be bombed. After all we had been through we did not want to be killed by our own airmen. Fortunately this did not happen.

The Allies began to advance beyond the Falaise Gap where they had been held up for some time and our hopes of being rescued began to rise. Lucien came daily with news mixed with rumour. It was very difficult to get a clear picture of what was happening and we began to get impatient. The Germans were retreating and we could hear fighting and gunfire all around us. Lucien told us to stay in the forest and impressed upon us that individuals should not try to go it alone as the danger of being picked up was very great. The retreating Germans would be at the forest in no time to shoot the lot of us. In spite of this warning one airman got impatient and left and we never heard from him again. Some were getting very restless and feared that if we stayed we would be discovered by the Germans anyway and we would be sitting ducks. However common sense prevailed and no one else left on their own. The hardest thing was the waiting. Lucien came daily and told us what he had heard about the position of the Allied troops but we waited in vain. All was largely rumour and we were getting yet more impatient. On occasions we heard shots being fired.

About 10 August, having heard that the Allies had reached Le Mans about 70 miles from the forest, Lucien decided to go there by car. Driven by Etienne Viron he went to try to make contact with the British Forces in order to get us away as soon as possible. By good luck after a long and dangerous trip he met the head of MI9, Airey Neave, and pressed upon him and the SAS the need to come and rescue us as soon as possible. Apparently there was a difficulty in obtaining transport. While they were away an American Jeep arrived in the forest with two GI's in it, having been told about us by some people in a near-by village. They then left to get some food for us and later returned loaded up with American food, spam, coffee and other goodies, and we enjoyed the best meal many of us had had for months.

The next day we received information that the Gestapo were in nearby Cloyes and that they were on their way to the forest. There was panic and we decided to scatter but as there was six of us as a crew we decided to stick together. Others went in small groups to nearby villages where the villagers were astonished to find themselves confronted by people speaking English. The six of us went into a village shop where we were given red wine and although there was no food there was a girl who could speak a little English. She went and got some eggs and made omelettes which we ate washing them down with red wine.

After that as it was late we decided to look for somewhere to sleep. We came to another village and found another shop where we were given yet more eggs and red wine. This time we had an audience of excited French men and women who kept giving us wine and patting us on the back. I think we paid for some of what we consumed because all of us had money from our escape packs on us. Having drunk to excess a farmer took us to his barn and we went to sleep in the hay. In the early hours of the morning we were awakened by the sound of heavy footsteps on the cobbles outside. We all froze but the footsteps died away to our great relief. We left the farm to return to the camp, thanking the farmer as we did so. As we made our way back to the forest we heard a motor cycle behind us getting closer. Once again I thought that even at this late stage 'we are going to get caught and not going to make it after all'. It was a tremendous relief when the rider called out in an American drawl "do any of you bastards speak English". He told us that an armoured convoy was on its way to the forest.

We went back to the forest for the last time. Lucien had just returned with Etienne Viron. They were both badly shaken, their car having overturned on the way back. They informed us of the difficulties and that it would be sometime before we could be rescued. However soon after Lucien had told us this a convoy of American trucks arrived with an escort of armed jeeps and armoured cars. Everyone began to scramble aboard. The skipper went to his spot in the forest and collected his parachute, a large part of which he had saved. It had been useful at night to sleep under and it was large enough for several of us to share. With the others I climbed aboard one of the trucks. Excitement continued however. There was the sound of gunfire all around us and as we were about to move off there was the sound of rifle fire. The American drivers and their mates grabbed their rifles and started firing and I thought we were all going to be caught up in the fighting and be killed, just as safety was looming up. However after a little while the firing died down and we moved off in the direction of Cloyes.

As we moved off we passed a convoy of busses all decked out with the Free French insignia and French flags. It was Airey Neave, head of MI9, who had come to rescue us. He was able to collect the remaining few in the two camps who had not got aboard the American vehicles. Airey Neave had arrived in Le Mans on 10 August equipped with half a dozen Jeeps and a few automatic weapons. Totally inadequate to effect the rescue of 150 airmen trapped in enemy territory when German battle groups were reported to be between Le Mans and Chateaudun. He needed transport to rescue the airmen. He did not know that the Americans would arrive with transport. He eventually found some civilian busses decked out with French flags and then mustered some drivers and set off for the forest, only to arrive after most of us had left on the American transport. That evening it was reported that German patrols were in the forest alerted by the activities and rejoicing in the area. If we had still been there we would undoubtedly been shot. And so ended our remarkable episode in the Forest of Freteval.

To have planned and executed a scheme to hide and feed 152 airmen under the noses of the German Army and the Gestapo was an outstanding achievement. Jean de Blomaert was awarded the DSO, since he had begun the camp, and had already done great service for the è Escape line. Lucien Boussa received the MC. They both received immediate awards as well as the French and Belgian Croix de Guerre. Omer Jubault and other members of Comète also received awards.

Escape lines Memorial weekend.
At Allandale, Ray and Rica's home, Leeds, May 2003
From left to right
Rica, Nadine, Lydier and her husband, Andre de la Lindi.

Resistance leader Omar Jubault
photographed at Freteval in April 1994
Left, the Royal Air Force Escaping Society
outside Brussels Town Hall, October 1997
Raymond Itterbeck, right, talking to *Franco*.

HOMEWARD BOUND

Chapter Ten

Meanwhile we continued through Cloyes towards Le Mans. On the way we stopped and were told by the drivers to keep our heads down as a suspicious car was parked at the side of the road. A couple of soldiers were sent to the car and each rolled a grenade under it. There was an explosion and we continued on our way. We camped for the night sleeping on the lorries, or on the ground beside. The next we day motored to Le Mans.

We reached Le Mans which had been liberated only a few days before and halted in the yard of an old French army barracks where we were given some American food. One of the outbuildings had been used as a store and the Germans in their haste to escape had left large quantities of their equipment behind. We took advantage of this to help ourselves to souvenirs. I helped myself to various objects, in particular a German helmet, but I had lost the lot, including the helmet, before I got home. We spent the night at Le Mans and the next day those 25 or so airmen who had been rescued by Airey Neave arrived to join us. They were then put on the American trucks and we all set off in the direction of Laval, passing through pockets of enemy territory.

On arriving at Laval the convoy drove into the city square where people were celebrating their liberation. Within seconds our trucks were surrounded and our drivers, although armed with sub machine guns, were helpless at keeping the crowds away from the trucks. We realised that the crowds thought that we were German prisoners and they were going to get their revenge. We were all in scruffy civilian clothes and any group of people of looking less like a bunch of RAF airmen is hard to imagine. Ken, our wireless operator, remarked "fancy getting this far only to be lynched by our friends". Fortunately, and in desperation, someone produced his RAF badges and we all shouted RAF and the ugly mood changed completely. In contrast we were offered wine and cigarettes.

After leaving Laval we headed north towards Bayeux on narrow winding roads. There were about six vehicles in the convoy and we drove very fast considering the state of the roads. I was in the back of the third truck and we approached a bend, which was sharper than it looked, very fast. The two leading vehicles negotiated it and ours just made it but had to swerve violently, and the vehicle behind us looked as if it was going to turn over. The vehicle after that lost control on the bend, hit the bank, and completely overturned. All in the back were flung out. We all stopped and went to try to help. There were bodies all over the place on the verges, on the road, but all alive. Two were trapped under the lorry but were released by getting a tree and levering the lorry off them. There was blood all over the place. The local people came and helped with bandages and put up the badly injured in their homes. Soon some American Army ambulances arrived and took the injured away. The rest, who were unhurt, crowded on to the remaining trucks and we took off in haste before the Germans, who were still in the area, arrived on the scene.

We journeyed on towards Bayeux. Somewhere short of the Falaise Gap we pulled into an American Camp which was full of German prisoners of all ranks captured during the fighting in that area. We were given a meal. There was no accommodation and so we had to sleep out in the open that night within a few yards of the wire netting behind which the German prisoners were being kept. We were each given a rifle with which to defend ourselves in case of a breakout. Fortunately it was a hot night, as it had been throughout my stay in France, so we did not come to any harm. When the Americans found out that we had a Russian with us they took him away in spite of our protestations andput him with the German prisoners and we never heard what had happened to him. We were sorry because he had been very cooperative and had done all the dirty work for us in the forest.

The next day we moved off towards Bayeux. All the way up the Normandy peninsular we passed great devastation, wrecked vehicles and equipment, dead animals and humans, bloated and swelling in the August heat. Towns and villages were reduced to a heap of rubble. We passed through St Lo. It had been completely destroyed and the only structure left standing was a solitary church spire. I drove through St Lo in 1994 on my way to a reunion at the Forest of Freteval, and St Lo had been completely rebuilt with not the slightest sign of any war damage. It was hard to believe it was the same place that I had passed through in 1944.

We arrived at Bayeux where we were handed over to the RAF intelligence who interrogated us, wanting to know all the details about what had happened to us, and what we had seen. We were given tented accommodation, and told that we would be flown home as soon as aircraft were available.

We were able to wash and have showers, a luxury that we had not enjoyed for weeks. Aircraft space was in short supply as all available aircraft were being used to fly the wounded back to the UK. We had to wait our turn and when space was available we were flown out in ones and twos. It was nearly a week before I got the chance to be flown home. I therefore spent a week killing time in Bayeux. There was little to do. Bayeux was badly damaged, but not destroyed like some of the towns and villages we had seen on the way. A few cafes were open but there was not much available other than coffee and cheap wine. One day Frank our rear gunner and I found a barber and we were able to have a much needed hair cut. But mainly it was just nice to be able to walk in the streets without the fear of being arrested.

One day I was informed that there was space for me on an aircraft bringing back the wounded. Two or three of us were found space on it amongst all the stretcher cases which were being put on board. Most of them not a pretty sight. I counted myself lucky I was not one of them.

We landed at RAF Northolt and were taken into London to the Air Ministry where we were again interrogated in detail about our experiences, and then accommodated for the night. The following day we were given leave which seemed almost too good to be true. The rest of the crew were there and we all went on our separate ways. We did not fly together again. Once an airman had successfully evaded capture by the Germans, it was RAF policy not to send him back on operations in the same theatre of war because it was felt that
if shot down he might not be so fortunate the second time and he might give away information that would compromise the escape routes and endanger the very people who had helped him. However, by the time I got back to England the advancing armies had largely eliminated the need for escape lines and this policy was not so strictly applied.

The pilot, navigator and bomb aimer were Australian and returned home. Ken, our wireless operator, went out and did a tour of operation in the Far East. Frank, the rear gunner, became an instructor. Sadly Tom, the other gunner, did not survive and remains buried in a cemetery in France. As for myself after a few weeks leave I was posted to Canada to join 45 Group Atlantic Transport Command at Dorval Airport Montreal, to fly Liberators and Lancasters which were being built in America and Canada, across the Atlantic to the UK, the Middle and the Far East.

1944

A PACKAGE HOLIDAY

Chapter Eleven

Early in October 1944 I was on the Queen Mary at Greenock on my way to Canada to join 45 Group Atlantic Transport Command at Dorval Airport Montreal. The Queen Mary was then a troop ship ploughing between America and the UK. It took 7 days to reach New York, taking an indirect course to avoid U boats lurking in the Atlantic. On board were Bing Crosby, Fred Astair and Bob Hope, returning from a tour of entertaining the American troops in Britain. Consequently we were treated to a show in the ships canteen every evening. Having seen them on the films many times it was a wonderful experience to see these stars performing in person at close quarters.

Early on the morning of the seventh day we passed the Statute of Liberty as we entered New York harbour. An impressive sight on a bright October morning with the skyscrapers towering in the background. When the Queen Mary docked we got a good idea of her size as we stood on deck and looked down on to the roofs of the warehouses and other large buildings on the dockside. We spent many hours before we were allowed to disembark. Then I with other airman bound for the same destination were transported to New York Grand Central Station. By then it was late afternoon and dark and as we drove through New York it was a blaze of light such as we had never seen before, and certainly not since 1939. There were no black out restrictions, which we had endured in the UK for the past five years.

New York Station was an impressive sight, clean and well lit compared to our dingy blacked out stations at home. We were able to indulge ourselves with cream doughnuts and other goodies from the trolleys on the platform provided by the Red Cross and other voluntary organisations. We finally got under way, and after an overnight train journey we drew into Montreal early the following morning. Montreal was to be my base for the next twelve months. Again, like New York, no sign of war, everywhere was lit up at night. No rationing, plenty of food in the shops and restaurants. We were billeted at an RCAF camp on the outskirts of Montreal. It was comfortable and the food was above the standard which I had been accustomed to, on any of my previous camps in the UK although we ate out much of the time.

Our base was to be Dorval Airport a few miles out of Montreal, to which we were taken every morning by bus which ran a shuttle service between the camp and the airport. We returned in the afternoon usually quite early. Dorval was for those times a large civilian airport into and out of which flew passenger planes from all parts of the American continent, the UK and elsewhere. Those coming from the UK were flown by BOAC. The aircraft were Liberators which had been converted to carry passengers, most of whom were VIP's, for in those days a permit was required to fly as a civilian passenger.

The RAF had a section of the airport from which we delivered new aircraft which had been built in the USA and Canada to the UK and also to the Middle and Far East. There was, of course, a range of aircraft which had to be delivered, from four engined bombers to twin engined aircraft such as Mosquitoes. Pilots had to familiarise themselves with a number of different aircraft types. As flight engineers we were only required on four engined aircraft which, for the most part, meant American Liberators and Lancasters which were being built in Ontario, with which we had to familiarise ourselves. After a week or so we were checked out on these. There was not much of a problem in so far as the Lancasters were concerned for most of us had flown in Lancaster and Halifax, but the Liberator was a very different type of aircraft. However most of us passed out successfully after a week or so and were therefore qualified to fly as flight engineers on both types.

Life was very exciting and very different from life on an RAF station at home. We were free from discipline. In fact we were more like civilian crews than RAF. We were required to report to the Flight Engineer Leader ie the officer in charge of flight engineers, every morning about 10am to see if we were required for a trip. If not we were free after lunch until the following day. Sometimes we were required to do a flight test. That is to go up for about an hours flight to ensure that everything was in working order. We had, therefore, plenty of spare time and there was plenty to do if you had the money. Montreal was a very vibrant city with restaurants nightclubs, bars and cinemas and some good service clubs run by organisations such as the YMCA, which, in Canada, was referred to as the "Y" club. There was one particularly good club. The Air Force Club run on a voluntary basis with facilities
such as lounges, a restaurant, bar and games room where you could always find RAF and Canadian aircrews. But Montreal was an expensive place although we were given extra pay in the form of a subsistence allowance to bring us up to the level of pay of the Canadian Air Force, which was considerably higher than RAF rates of pay.

TRANS ATLANTIC

Chapter Twelve

After two or three weeks I was told that I would be required for a trip and that I was to report for briefing at 15.30 hours. In the briefing room I met the other members of the crew with whom I was going to fly. The Captain was a civilian, an American who had flown as an airline pilot before the war. The co-pilot, navigator and myself were RAF and the wireless operator was Canadian a civilian. At briefing we learned that we were to ferry a new American Liberator to Prestwick in Scotland. This was the base to which we delivered all aircraft which were destined for the United Kingdom and from where they would be collected by the RAF, fitted up for operational duties at a maintenance unit and then delivered on to the squadrons. Prestwick was the first available airfield when coming in from the Atlantic.

It was now the beginning of November 1944 and we were told at briefing that the weather was too bad to fly the customary Northern route which meant refuelling at Goose Bay in Labrador or at Gander in Newfoundland, before crossing the Atlantic. In those days we did not carry enough fuel to fly the Atlantic direct. We would therefore be taking the Southern route refuelling at Bermuda and the Azores and then to Prestwick. This meant an early take off and we were required to report at 6am the following morning. Back at the billet I set the alarm for an early call and proceeded to pack my kit. As this was my first trip it was a problem knowing just what to take. I had to allow for the fact that I would be living out of a suit case, or rather a kit bag, for the next ten days or so. I had to think what would be required.

On landing at Prestwick we were required to make arrangements for returning to Dorval. There were three ways of getting back. First we could be booked on the BOAC
flight, the passengers being VIP's and returning ferry crews. The aircraft used were Liberators flown by BOAC which had been converted for civilian use. There was usually a waiting list which meant that we would be given accommodation for a night or two in the transit wing. If there was a waiting list of say four or five days we could be given a pass to go home, which I took advantage of, on more than one occasion. The second way of returning was to be given a warrant to Liverpool or Greenock where we would board one of the boats sailing to New York or Halifax, Nova Scotia. This was not a popular way of returning because the boat trip could take up to seven days followed by a train journey of two or three days. I once went back this way, travelling by train to Liverpool then boarding the Pasteur, an old uncomfortable French

ship. This took seven days before docking at Halifax, followed by a train journey which took two nights and two days before it reached Montreal. Needless to say we got ourselves on the BOAC flight whenever we could.

The third way was to go to Largs on the Clyde from where there was a flying boat service run by the Royal Canadian Air Force which landed on the St Lawrence river near Montreal. During the course of twelve months I travelled all three ways.

Next morning after an early breakfast we took off from Dorval and set course for Bermuda. After about four and a half hours flying we landed on Bermuda. As it was the first week in November it was cold when we took off from Montreal but landing at Bermuda it was, by contrast, a warm summers day with the temperature in the 70's. The weather report for the South Atlantic being bad we stayed overnight at the airfield which was run by the Americans.

During the afternoon some of us decided to view the Island. The airfield was on a strip of land just off the main island. We took the boat across the narrow strip of water in lovely warm sunshine. The sea was warm and very blue. Ashore we took the little train to Hamilton, the capital, passing on the way fields full of beautiful flowers which gave off a lovely flagrance. There was no pollution on Bermuda because there was no industry there, and the only motor vehicles permitted were those used by the American Air Force. Apart from a little railway the only transport on the island was horse drawn. We spent the rest of the day in Hamilton, a lovely small town. No hustle and bustle and only the sound of horse drawn vehicles to disturb the peace. We spent the evening visiting various bars and then took a horse drawn carriage to a lovely hotel on the edge of the town overlooking the sea and set amongst pine trees. It was a warm calm night and with the moon shining on the water one could not have wished for a more romantic setting, although we were not able to take advantage of this. Later we made our way back to the airfield ready for take off in the morning on the next leg of our journey.

We took off from Bermuda the following morning wishing we could have stayed longer, and set course for the Azores, a long flight of over 2000 miles. In those days it was about ten hours flying time, with nothing to see but sea and sky. We did not fly high crossing the Atlantic, staying between 7,000 and 10,000 feet. That meant that we were much more dependent on the weather than modern aircraft which can fly above the storms. After about 10 hours the peaks of one of the islands (there are nine of them) appeared out of the sea. This was a great relief because we did not have much fuel left and there was nowhere else to land if the navigator had made an error.

The airfield, a staging post run by the Americans, was on the main island. It was set between hills which made landing difficult, particularly if visibility was bad. This was the cause of one or two accidents. We were accommodated in the transit mess for the night. It was very warm but unlike Bermuda it was very humid and damp and not pleasant. We took off again the next evening in darkness. The airfield was merely a landing strip from which aircraft took off and came in over the sea, there being as far as I can remember only one runway which was made out of wire mesh rather like thick wire fencing. This made a metallic sound as the aircraft went over it. We set course for Prestwick, again a distance of about 2000 miles, and some 9 to 10 hours flying time away.

A PASSAGE TO INDIA

Chapter Thirteen

On arriving over Prestwick there was mist and low cloud and we were diverted to Dyce, an RAF airfield on the East coast near Aberdeen, which was clear of fog. After a few hours at Dyce we got the all clear and took off again to Prestwick where we landed some fifteen minutes later. On reporting to movements we were told that they could not get us on a return flight and that we would have to wait at least 24 hours. The following day while waiting for a seat on BOAC flight I was approached in the bar by another crew. They were en route to India to deliver a Liberator but their flight engineer had been taken ill. They asked me if I would be willing to join the crew. The idea appealed to me but as I had only expected to be away from Dorval about a week, and as this would mean I should be away for a further two weeks at least, I was going to be short of clothing and other personal items. However, as this looked like an interesting trip I agreed. The captain was a civilian, an Australian who had been a commercial pilot in America for many years. The co-pilot was a young RCAF pilot, the navigator was like myself RAF and the radio operator was a Canadian civilian who had had a considerable amount of flying experience in America and Canada. A mixed bunch, but we soon got on well together as one does when working closely in a team.

We took off the following morning. The first stop was Malta for refuelling. We flew over France, then in Allied hands, and we got a clear and impressive view of Mont Blanc to our east as we flew at about 7000 feet. Flying at those heights one got an interesting view of the landscape over which one was flying, in contrast to modern jet aircraft, up at 30,000 feet, where one sees very little of the land below. It was an interesting contrast to me, having been on bomber command where most of the flying was done at night, the only scenery being search lights, anti aircraft fire and tracer from night fighters. It was also a relief not to be in fear of being attacked. We flew on to Malta where we landed after dark, having flown over 1800 miles in about 9 hours. Here we refuelled, had a meal and after a few hours rest we departed for Cairo, a distance of about 1200 miles, and a flight of just over 6 hours.

Dawn was just breaking as we approached the RAF airfield, and coming in low to land we got a magnificent view of the pyramids, quite breath-taking when seen for the first time from the air. We were to stay the night here not having had much sleep during the past 24 hours. After a short rest myself and another member of the crew got a lift on the back of an RAF vehicle which was going into Cairo. We spent the afternoon and early evening sight seeing before returning to the camp for the night. Cairo was hot, humid, dusty and busy. It was also full of British service people, mostly army.

The next day we were due to take off on the next stage of the journey which would take us over Iraq and Iran, with a stop at RAF base Shibah, in Iraq. Then on to Karachi, then in India, now in Pakistan. However the following day the weather report was bad with heavy storms en route up to about 15000 feet. The skipper was anxious to take off, having no desire to spend another day in Cairo, having been many times before. He pointed out that we could fly over the storm as the Liberator was capable of climbing to 20000 feet or more. But this aircraft had not had oxygen apparatus fitted and the RAF members of the crew, having had it drilled into us that it was unsafe to fly above 10000 feet without oxygen, refused. After some argument the skipper gave in but said he was going to find another route. He returned from flying control and said we were going to fly via Aden and then over the Indian Ocean and on to Karachi.

We took off from Cairo for Aden, a distance of about 1500 miles and about 7 hours flying time. We flew over the Suez Canal and then over the Red Sea. After about 5 hours I noticed that one of the fuel gauges was reading very low and we would have insufficient fuel to reach Aden. The nearest landing ground was Asmara and so we called up and got permission to land. Asmara was in what then was Italian Eritrea otherwise Abyssinia and it was an RAF staging post. It was not a very well equipped staging post and we were the first four engined aircraft to land there. However they promised to examine the fuel tanks and system for leaks but it would take some time, and so we were found overnight accommodation on the camp.

That evening three of us went into the town. A nondescript place as far as I can remember. We had a meal of tough steak in a restaurant and then had a walk round the town. There were Americans everywhere. We passed a brothel where there were two American soldiers on duty outside! It was apparently approved by the American authorities. Our co-pilot, a young Canadian recently married, was missing his wife and decided to have a go. The navigator and myself were too timid to risk it and continued to look round the town. We met up with our colleague later. He said he had enjoyed the experience and that he would go again the next night if we were still there. He said that when he had finished the session he was given an anti-syphilis jab by an American medical orderly who was on duty. We then got transport back to the camp.

The following morning the ground crew told us that they had examined the petrol tanks and the fuel system and could find nothing wrong and that it had been a false alarm due to a faulty petrol gauge. Liberator petrol gauges were prone to inaccuracy. Hoping that they were right we prepared for take off with some trepidation because the runway was not very long. It was made of wire mesh, and further, Asmara was situated about 8000 feet above sea level which reduced the lift. Also, the airfield was surrounded by mountains. However with full power we managed to get airborne just before the end of the runway and got over the mountains with a little room to spare and set course for Aden - a distance of about 500 miles and about three hours flying time.

We landed at Aden soon after midday. The heat was intense. We were given billets and all we wanted to do was to lie on our beds with the large electric fan whirling above us. The camp was largely occupied by the Americans who, that evening, were to be entertained by Phyllis Dixie the well known English fan dancer. At the time she was doing a tour entertaining the troops in that part of the world. I was so hot and tired that I did not go to see her perform. I waited until after the war when I saw her at the Leeds City Varieties to which she was a regular visitor.

We took off in the early hours of the following morning bound for Karachi, a distance of about 1,600 miles or eight hours flying time. The route took us out over the Gulf of Aden, the Indian Ocean and the Arabian Sea to Karachi where we landed some eight hours later, again in intense heat almost as oppressive and humid as it had been in Aden. Karachi was normally our destination and we left the aircraft there to be collected by the squadron for whom it was destined. Ferry crews then waited until there was a seat on an RAF transport aircraft which would take us back to the UK to RAF Lineham in Wiltshire. From there they would travel by train to Prestwick and then by BOAC back to Montreal. That was the normal routine. However the skipper, being a civilian pilot, and not therefore subject to RAF authority, decided that he would like to visit Calcutta, never having been there.

After arguing with flying control he got their authority for us to deliver the aircraft to the squadron to which it was destined rather than the usual procedure which was for them to collect it from Karachi. We were provided with accommodation for the night and that evening we all went into the town where we went to the Bristol Hotel and had a superb Indian meal, the first Indian food I had ever had and probably better than I have had since. We left the hotel about 11pm to get a taxi back to the airfield.

While waiting for the taxi on this warm clear Indian night with the bright moon and the stars above I was struck by how calm and still it was and how unreal and remote it all seemed, like an *Alice in Wonderland* story or, more appropriately, *Arabian Nights.* Only five months before I was hiding in a forest in France expecting to be caught and shot, and eight months ago I was at the beginning of a tour on Bomber Command being attacked and seeing aircraft going down in flames. Now I had just had a meal in a luxury hotel in India (now Pakistan) and to get here I had flown long distances across continents and oceans, albeit far from the danger of attack. On the other hand the engines have to keep going, when flying over oceans, deserts and mountains, as a parachute is not much help. There are no resistance helpers in such uninhabited regions to provide food and shelter. I thought how lucky I was to be having a great experience with more to come. Life can be good but you have to survive to enjoy it.

The squadron to which we were to take the aircraft was based near Allahabad about nine hundred miles east from Karachi in central India, a journey of about four and a half hours. The skipper deviated off course to Agra to enable us all to see the Taj Mahl. We came down to about five hundred feet to get a good look and the skipper flew over it several times to allow those with a camera to take photographs. I had my camera with me and took several shots but sadly later in my travels lost the camera, which was a pity because it would have been wonderful to have had photographs of this magnificent building from the air, regarded as the most beautiful building in the world. We flew on to Allahabad where we booked into an hotel, after which myself and the navigator had a look round the town, a University town, a seat of the High Court. It was the centre of the Nationalist movement under British rule and home of the Nehru family.

We looked at the shops. There were many jewellery shops and we went into one or two. I remember the proprietor of one spoke excellent English and was very well educated. I was surprised how much English was spoken in this rather distant outpost of the empire. Back in the hotel I had a large room to myself and a big bed surrounded in mosquito netting, but it did not prevent me from getting one or two nasty bites.

The next morning a short flight took us to the squadron on an airfield out in the jungle where we were to leave the aircraft. It was a Canadian squadron and they all assumed that we were a new crew posted in. They began to commiserate with us until they discovered who we were, and that we had reached our destination, and that after lunch we were returning to Canada. They were very envious, especially as it was the end of November and that we would be back in Canada for Christmas. Our next task was to get to Calcutta to catch the RAF transport going back to the UK. We were informed that there was a shuttle service to Calcutta and that the Dakota was due in shortly and so after a quick lunch, the Dakota having arrived, we collected our kit, said our good byes, and scrambled aboard the aircraft. As we were leaving some of the Canadians gave us their Christmas letters home asking us to post them when we got back, saying that they would reach their families and friends sooner than if posted through the normal post.

An hour and a half later we landed at Dum Dum airport, Calcutta. On checking in we were told that there was an RAF transport Liberator departing for the UK at 3am on which there were five seats available. As it was then early afternoon we decided that rather than hang around the

76

airport we would view the sights of Calcutta. We collected our kit, hired a taxi (a 1920's Ford) into which we managed to get all our kit, including the five of us. Making the taxi heavily overloaded we set off for Calcutta. We booked in at the air terminal where we left our kit and set off to view the sights. We were able to buy such things as silk stockings which were unobtainable in the UK at the time although by this time I had become use to seeing such merchandise available in Canada. What struck me was the amount of fruit available of all kinds. Oranges, lemons, pears melons etc being sold on the market stalls and by street traders. I decided that on the chance of being able to call at home on the way back to Prestwick I would buy a large basket of tangerines, unseen in England since the beginning of the war, as a Christmas present for my parents. I bought a large basket of six dozen and left them at the air terminal to be collected when we returned. We toured the bars, had a good evening meal after which we spent the evening in a night club, drinking such drinks as "John Collins", a mixture of gin, lemonade and sugar.

Sometime after midnight we made our way back to the air terminal in a very inebriated state collected our baggage and got transport back to the airport and checked in. Our baggage, which including my tangerines, was taken and put into the hold of the aircraft. Sadly when we arrived in the UK they were so squashed as to be not worth eating.

On checking, in the rest of the passengers, including a number of high ranking officers who had checked in ahead of us, were making their way to the aircraft. Our skipper, full of fun and drink, decided that we should play a game and pretend that we were the crew that were to fly the aircraft. We walked out to the aircraft singing and rolling about. This alarmed the passengers one of whom, a senior army officer, got out of his seat saying that he was not going to travel in an aircraft flown by a load of drunks and that he was going to report us to higher authority. This caused quite a stir amongst the rest of the passengers, and voices were raised. However the matter was settled amicably when the crew who were to fly the aircraft came out and explained that we were not the crew who were to fly the aircraft but a ferry crew returning as passengers!

We landed at Karachi where some passengers got off and others got on and then flew on and landed at Sheiba in the Persian Gulf for refuelling, and then to Cairo. At Cairo we stayed for several hours where the aircraft was refuelled and serviced and this gave us time to get off the aircraft and have a proper meal and stretch our legs. From Cairo we flew to Malta where we landed and had time to get a meal in the transit mess after which we took off flying over the Mediterranean Sea and then over France.

It was daylight as we flew low over France, which was now safely clear of Germans, who had by then retreated. It was difficult to believe that six months earlier when flying over the same territory we were being attacked by anti aircraft fire and fighters, and that six months earlier I had been hiding from the Germans in a forest not far from the area over which we were now flying. I looked down on a typical December day, grey wet and windy, a compete contrast to the tropical weather I had been experiencing a few hours earlier. We landed at Lineham in Wiltshire from where we had to make our way back to Prestwick with a rail pass. I telephoned Prestwick and was told that the BOAC flights were heavily booked and if anyone wanted a few days leave they could have it. I took the opportunity and so had a few days at home en route minus, unhappily, the tangerines which I had bought.

Each morning I telephoned Prestwick from home to see if there was a seat for me. It was like being on standby in today's parlance and there was no seat available until on the fourth day when I rang I was told I had been booked on an aircraft for the following day. I had been lucky to get a few days leave which did not come off my annual allowance but now I had to endure a long train journey in overcrowded wartime trains. After about nine hours I arrived at Prestwick late at night to fly out the following day. I had become accustomed to travelling 2,000 miles in that time. The next day I boarded a BOAC Liberator bound for Montreal. These Liberators were converted for passenger use and carried about twenty. They were fitted with extra large fuel tanks to enable them to fly non stop to Montreal, over fifteen hours flying time. I had a window seat and about two hours after take off I noticed streaks of liquid across the window, and it was clearly oil. I attracted the attention of the steward. There was only one. He went and got the flight engineer who, when he saw it, said he would have to report it to the captain. The next thing was an announcement from the Captain that we were turning back. We returned to Prestwick where we spent several hours in the departure lounge before the fault was corrected and we took off again and landed at Dorval with no further trouble.

It was now the middle of December. I had been away just over three weeks and the climate had changed since my departure. It was snowing and the ground was completely covered, and it remained like this until Easter. It was very cold in contrast to the tropical weather I had just recently experienced and I was glad to get back to my billet and get into my great coat and winter underwear.

The contrast between flying on Bomber Command and Transport Command could not have been greater. The reader only has to compare my first trip on Bomber Command with this latter, my first trip on Transport Command. On Transport Command when we took off we could expect to reach our destination. It is true that there were accidents, particularly in winter, over the north Atlantic, with aircraft getting iced up, or occasionally due to engine failure, but these were exceptions. On Bomber Command one faced danger as soon as one crossed the enemy coast, until it was crossed again on the way back, as well as the other hazards.

On the other hand ferry crews faced long flights over sea and barren territory, often boring and arduous. It was not unusual to be airborne for eleven hours or more, whereas on Bomber Command six hours would be a long trip. On Bombers you took off and returned to the same base. Transport aircraft flew on, stopping at many places on the way, and in many different countries. You had to adapt to constant changes of climate from one extreme to another in the course of one trip. Sometimes, after a long leg, you might have only a short break before proceeding on another long leg of the journey. Sometimes, due to weather or other circumstances, you might have a stop over of several days.

Also, you passed through many time zones, kept irregular hours, had irregular meals, and often eating while airborne. Again, you never flew with the same crew twice, and crews were usually mixed crews, civilian and RAF. The civilian men were often older with different backgrounds and experience. On Bombers you kept the same crew for a whole tour and you got to know them and understand their reactions in different circumstances. On Transport you had to adapt to different personalities and temperaments on each trip. Although lacking the dangers of Bomber Command all this imposed strain on an airman, and we were always ready for our leave, after each trip.

THE ATLANTIC AGAIN

Chapter Fourteen

After a trip to the Middle or Far East we were entitled to five days leave. After a trip to the UK three days. This was in addition to our annual leave of seven days every three months. I was now therefore free to idle my time for five days during which time I was able to do my Christmas shopping from the wide range of merchandise available in the shops and stores. The civilian population were very hospitable and over Christmas there were plenty of invitations to parties. The Air Force Club and the YMCA which I attended gave a very good Christmas lunch and party. I was not required for a trip again until after the New Year and so I was able to enjoy New Year in Montreal. On New Years Eve I was invited to the Montreal Athletic Club for a meal, party and dance. This was a club to join if you lived in Montreal, it being well equipped for sport including an indoor pool and excellent catering facilities.

A few days into the New Year I was required for another trip. It was to deliver another Liberator to Prestwick. We took off from Dorval and flew to Goose Bay, an RAF staging post near the coast in Labrador. This was about a four hour flight over largely uninhabited territory, almost all forest, with the whole landscape covered in snow. Mile after mile of snow, making me realise what a vast country Canada is. Goose Bay was a staging post set in an area clear of trees. It was very flat with long runways and plenty of space for taking off and landing. It was miles from anywhere and very cold and bleak. It was staffed by RAF and Canadian ground crews who were stationed there. I was glad I was not one of them. It was dark soon after we landed. We were given a meal and accommodation for the night.

The next day the Skipper, an American civilian, and the navigator went for a briefing and as there were strong tail winds they decided we could fly direct to Prestwick, an estimated flight time of over twelve hours. I was having to get used to long distance flying. The more usual route was to fly from Montreal to Gander in Newfoundland and from there the shorter hop to Prestwick. We had flown the previous day over snow covered forests and bleak landscape. I now had to experience flying for many hours over sea. If the previous days landscape was bleak this was even bleaker. We flew at nine thousand feet from west to east and there was no relief to the monotonous sight of sky and sea, hour after hour after hour. Occasionally we would catch sight of a lone weather ship anchored in the Atlantic, placed there to transmit weather reports. After so many hours over the sea it was a relief to land at Prestwick and get ones feet on terra firma.

On this trip I tried my hand at smuggling. I had brought with me 750 Lucky Strike cigarettes, unobtainable in the UK where cigarettes were in short supply. This was above the tax free limit of 200. It was common practice for crews to bring cigarettes for friends and relations. Mine were intended as a present for my father in the hope that I might get a few days stand-by leave before returning to Montreal. Failing that I would post them to him. However as we were getting off the plane were told that customs were having a check and we would have to go through customs, which normally we did not have to do. In panic I returned to the cockpit and left the cigarettes there. I passed through customs with nothing to declare and checked in and proceeded to the bar. Much relieved I was having a drink with the rest of the crew when a customs officer entered the bar and asked if we were the crew of Liberator B519 because 750 cigarettes had been found in the cockpit. I did not dare own up and the rest of the crew denied any knowledge of them. "Well, if no one owns them," said the customs officer, "I will confiscate 550 and distribute the 200 between you". As a result I finished up with 40 cigarettes out of 750!

As there were seats available on the BOAC Liberator the following day after one night in Prestwick I returned to Montreal. A direct flight of over15 hours.

As on returning from a UK trip I was allowed three days leave. I decided to try some skiing. The Laurentian Mountains lie about 60 miles east of Montreal, and, like the Lake District, they are a beauty spot. In the winter they are covered with snow until about Easter and are a ski resort - a miniature Switzerland. I booked in at a small hotel and took the train and spent three days there, my first experience on skis. The nursery slopes were on the golf course and the instructor was the golf professional who doubled as a ski instructor in the winter. The hotel was full of Americans and Canadians. It was an interesting and enjoyable short break.

NORTHERN IRELAND

Chapter Fifteen

On returning to Montreal I reported daily at the airport and apart from an occasional flight test I was not required. After a week or so I met an RAF pilot with whom I had been at school. He was going on a course for pilots in Northern Ireland and there was also a parallel course there for flight engineers. Both courses, I was told, were of three weeks duration. A Dakota required delivering to the UK and he was to fly it across, he had a navigator and a wireless operator who would return on reaching Prestwick and he would proceed on two weeks leave then go on the course at the end of which he would get a further weeks leave before returning to Montreal. He suggested that I might like to get myself on the flight engineers course and do the same and although Dakotas did not normally carry a flight engineer he could arrange to have one on this occasion. I thought that this was a good idea and so I made the necessary arrangements and got myself on the course.

We took off from Dorval early in the morning and flew to Goose Bay, Labrador, where we stayed overnight, and the following day took off for Gander, Newfoundland. Here we found the weather bad and had to stay for two nights before the weather improved sufficiently to allow us to take off on the next stage which meant going via the Azores for a rest and refuelling and from there to the UK landing in the South to refuel and then to Prestwick where we handed over the aircraft and reported to movements.

The navigator and wireless operator were returning to Canada but they managed to get a few days leave before doing so. The pilot was told that his course would not be starting for ten days and so proceeded on leave. As luck would have it I was told that my course was starting right away, it being of five weeks duration, not three, and so was given a warrant and told to report to the Royal Liver building in Liverpool from where I was given a passage on an overcrowded ferry to Belfast where we docked in the early hours of a Sunday morning. I then proceeded to RAF Nutts Corner to begin my course. On arrival I met a Canadian pilot, Louis Greenburgh, who had been hiding with me in the Forest of Freteval. He had been posted to Nutts Corner as a pilot instructor. He was the first person I had met since escaping from the forest who had been there with me and we had a lot to talk about.

After ten days the pilot arrived from leave to attend his course while I continued with mine for another three weeks. This was January/February 1945, a very severe winter when the sea around the coast froze in places. It was perishingly cold in Northern Ireland with no heat in the billets. Several nights I was so cold that I went to sleep in my flying kit. I regretted volunteering for the course as I could have been enjoying the comforts of Canada or seeing the world on a more interesting trip.

At the end of three weeks we were given a weeks leave after which we were to report to Liverpool. We embarked on the Pasteur, a French ship, already mentioned and which took a full seven days to cross the Atlantic. She was smaller and less comfortable than my crossing the previous October on the Queen Mary. It took us to Halifax, Novia Scotia, along with other ferry crews of which there were quite a number returning to Dorval. On disembarking we transferred to the train for the journey to Montreal which took over two days. The train was slow but comfortable. There was an observation lounge and a dining car which served good food and at night the steward came along and tipped up our seats which he then made up into berths. It was an interesting journey but I had had enough after two days and was glad when we arrived back in Montreal.

In the meantime my commission, which I had applied for back in June on the squadron, came through. It had taken a long time for my documents to catch up with me. That meant I had to get measured for my officers uniform. It also meant moving out of my billet in the camp at Lachine just outside Montreal and looking for digs. There was no officers accommodation either on the camp or at Dorval and so I had to look for civilian digs for which we were given an allowance to cover the cost. I found a room in the centre of Montreal there were two other air crew in the same house. The land lady did not provide food so it was necessary to eat out and of course there was plenty of choice in the way of restaurants and cafes although eating out was expensive. The landlady charged rent when we were away on trips so that the room was kept for us until we returned.

NORTH AFRICA

Chapter Sixteen

After about a week I was off on another trip. This time to deliver a Liberator to Algiers Maison Blanc airfield. We took off early morning and flew to Bermuda for an overnight stop and then to the Azores from where we flew to Rabat in Morocco, a distance of about 1000 miles. About four and a half hours flying time. On this occasion I had decided to try my hand at a little more smuggling, having been unsuccessful on the previous attempt with the cigarettes at Prestwick. It was possible in Canada to buy cheap watches, fountain pens jewellery and items of clothing such as shirts and underwear and to sell that at grossly inflated prices in North Africa. A lot of aircrew did it and got away with it. Before leaving I had bought a spare wrist watch, a fountain pen and a couple of shirts. These could be sold for five or six times the price paid in Canada. We landed at Rabat. Unfortunately to get out of the Liberator it was necessary to lower oneself from the hatch in the nose of the aircraft and jump down. In doing so my wrist hit the side of the hatch and smashed the watch, rendering it worthless. However I still had two shirts and a fountain pen to sell.

We were to stay overnight and so we were transported into Rabat where we were booked into an hotel. I had been told that the procedure was to go out of the back door of the hotel when, almost invariably, you would be approached by someone asking if you had anything to sell. I was warned to take care because the authorities were getting wise to what aircrews were doing and were on the look out. In fact one or two aircrew had been caught and taken into custody.

In my hotel room I unpacked and stuffed two shirts into the blouse of my battledress. I made for the rear exit of the hotel where, just before the exit door, was a bar and as I passed I noticed two men sitting on stools at the bar. One of them was sitting obliquely from where he could observe anyone passing along the passage. I thought this was a bit suspicious and so when outside in the street after I had walked about fifty yards I looked round to see if I was being followed. I saw the man I had seen in the bar about fifty yards behind me. I continued walking and was soon approached by a young lad who asked me if had anything to sell. Before saying yes I looked round again and saw that the man had stopped and was looking in a shop window. I decided not to take any risk and replied that I had nothing to sell. He did not believe me and insisted that I had something to sell. He was very persistent. I continued to deny that I had anything to sell and in the end he gave up and went away. He could not understand my attitude, as it must have been obvious that I had intended to do business. I looked round again to see the man who had followed me going back to the hotel. Looking back on this incident I am glad I did what I did because if I had made a sale I am sure I would have been arrested. I made no more attempts at smuggling!

The following day we took off for Algiers and landed some three hours later at Maison Blanc airfield to where the aircraft was to be delivered. This was an RAF airfield but it had been occupied by the Italians during their North African campaign. We were accommodated in the transit quarters which were quite comfortable but the heat was unbearably hot and the food was not very good. We were told that we would be here for a day or two until arrangements could be made to get us back to Canada.

During the afternoon I went into Algiers with another member of the crew. The whole place looked shabby dusty and dirty suffering from the effects of war. It had been variously occupied by the Italians, the Germans and now by the Americans and the British. While walking down one of the busy main streets I was accosted by two small boys, one of whom attempted to sell me a local newspaper, and while my attention was thus diverted the other little lad jumped up and plucked from the breast pocket of my battledress tunic the fountain pen I had brought to sell at a profit. They both ran off. This was the last of my contraband and it finally convinced me that smuggling was not for me.

The next day with two other members of the crew and a few RAF stationed at Maison Blanc we went into Algiers again. They who were stationed there wore their tropical kit which we crew members did not have. As it was very hot we took off our jackets and rolled up our sleeves. As such we were, of course, improperly dressed but as this was North Africa and we were thousands of miles from our base we thought nothing of it. Suddenly there was a screeching of brakes and an RAF jeep with two RAF police in it came to an abrupt halt. The two policemen came over to us and told us that we were improperly dressed and that they would be reporting us to our station commander. They asked us which unit we were from and when we said 45 Group Dorval, Canada, they did not believe us and thought we were being truculent, particularly as we were accompanied by the others who were stationed locally and properly dressed. When we showed them our documents to prove it they said they would be reporting us anyhow. Needless to say we heard nothing further about this incident. After a meal and quite a lot of drinks in Algiers we all went to a night club and saw a show which, even by present day standards, was very pornographic.

The following day our return journey had been arranged. We were flown in an RAF Dakota to Casablanca where we were booked on to an US Army Air Transport DC 54 Skymaster for the return trip. Taking off from Casablanca we flew direct to Bermuda just for refuelling and then to New York La Guardia which was then new York's Airport. We had to wait there for a few hours before we could get a seat on a Colonial Airways flight to Dorval. This was a Canadian airline which flew a regular service between New York and Montreal, a flight of about one and a half hours. We had to wait there an hour or two for the flight to Montreal, during which time I walked on to the airfield and watched a young girl of about 16 years learning to fly a small plane. The instructor got out and she went off solo. It all seemed to be quite casual, just like learning to drive. I could not imagine that happening at the time in the UK, at least not in 1945. The only indication here of a war was that the number of civilian flights had been reduced somewhat. This meant there were queues to get seats. However returning aircrews were given priority and so I went, with others, to the head of the queue. This upset a number of business men who complained that they had an important meeting to attend in Montreal. It made no difference. I still had priority. The only urgent matter which I had to deal with in Montreal was to claim my five days leave to which I was entitled. Understandably, they were annoyed. Soon after this it was Easter and the thaw began to melt the snow which had covered the ground since December. Also the ice on the St Lawrence river melted. Temperatures got very low in the winter in this part of Canada, but very warm, in the summer.

Soon after Easter I was on another trip this time to take a Liberator to Prestwick. After an early morning take off we flew to Newfoundland where we refuelled and then the long hop to Prestwick. We had to stay two nights before we could get a return flight. It was double British Summer time which was very noticeable in the North of Scotland and daylight remained until late. It had been a bright day and I was struck by the fact that it was still daylight when I walked back to my billet at midnight.

The next day we were booked on a BOAC Liberator. These aircraft were fitted with extra fuel tanks which enabled them to fly direct to Montreal without refuelling. The journey took about fifteen hours which was a long time in an aircraft less comfortable than present modern airliners, with no opportunity to stretch ones legs. By this time the war in Europe was coming to an end and we were about half way across the Atlantic at 10,000 feet when we heard that the Germans had surrendered. By the time we landed the news had reached Montreal and the whole place was in chaos. Everybody had stopped work and gone off to celebrate. It was difficult to get checked in because there was no one on duty. I managed to complete the formalities and then had difficulty getting transport into Montreal. I eventually managed to board an overcrowded bus with all my kit, which took me into the city, but it dropped me off some distance from my digs. Montreal was thronging with people. The bunting and streamers were out and I had difficulty making my way through the crowded streets with my kit to my digs. I made it at last, tired and dishevelled, after my journey. However after a wash and change I felt refreshed and went out to join in the celebrations.

Soon after this I did a further trip to Prestwick and on the return I had my first and only experience of flying in flying boats. The RAF had two American built flying boats which were stationed at Montreal on the St Lawrence river and which were used for passengers and returning ferry crews. We were transported to Largs, North of Prestwick, on the coast. We then flew to Iceland where we landed at Reykjavik for refuelling and a short break, and then to Montreal where we landed on the St Lawrence and were taken ashore by motor boat. Quite an experience.

Soon after getting back from this last trip I had the chance to go on a three week course at an American Airforce Camp close to Boston in the United States. 45 Group had a special squadron at Dorval equipped with Liberators which had been converted for carrying passengers and were used mainly for VIP work. However these were to be replaced with a few American C54 Skymasters. These were four engined aircraft which looked rather like a large Dakota. They had been built as passenger carrying aircraft and were used extensively by the US Army Air Transport for carrying troops. As no one in the RAF had had any experience of these planes it was decided to send about eight flight engineers on a course. This not only opened the prospect of an interesting three weeks at an American Air Force base but also that we would spending the rest of the war flying important personages round the world, an interesting prospect.

The base was a large one in the middle of the New Hampshire countryside. Very wooded and attractive like Hampshire in England from whence, presumably, it took it's name. Unlike England it was very hot, day after day, at that time of the year, June. There was a large lake within walking distance of the camp where we went to cool off in our free time. The camp was very comfortable with good food and I enjoyed my three weeks there doing circuits and bumps and short flights to familiarise ourselves with the Skymaster. At the end of the course we returned to Dorval and went back onto Liberators. We were told that the RAF were not going to get Skymasters after all. We understood that the reason was because the war in Europe was over. The course had therefore been unnecessary but, from my point of view, it had been an enjoyable experience.

A SECOND PASSAGE TO INDIA

Chapter Seventeen

A few days after my return from the States I made another trip to deliver a Liberator to Prestwick and returned by BOAC. Soon after this I was off to India again. The war in Europe now over, most of the trips were to deliver aircraft, usually Liberators, to the Far East. Further it had been decided that as air crews finishing their training in Canada would not be required in Europe anymore they would be posted straight to the Far East and that the quickest and easiest way to do this would be to let them fly their own aircraft out there. However as most flight engineers were trained in England and were then posted to the Far East the crews finishing training in Canada did not have an engineer in the crew. This problem was solved by one of us flying as part of the crew. Having hitherto flown with experienced civilian and RAF crews I was now to fly with a crew straight from training with no experience. In RAF parlance a "sprog crew" and also of course air gunners were part of the crew.

I attended briefing the day before take off when I met the new crew. All NCO'S and all Canadians except the two pilots who were English. It was a daunting experience especially for the skipper to find himself having to fly long distances over strange territory soon after training. We took off for Newfoundland and then to the Azores. A difficult landing and take off for an inexperienced pilot. From the Azores we flew to Rabat where we had an overnight stay. After booking into the hotel and a meal we all went out for the evening visiting several bars and sampling the various drinks on offer. Having been there previously I was able to act as guide.

The next day we took off and flew to Castel Benito an airfield on the coast in Libya, it had been used by the Italians during Mussolini's Libyan campaign during the early part of the war. In fact I think it was named after one of his sons-in-law who was in command of the Italian Air Force at the time. We were put up in the camp in quite comfortable billets, the camp now being run by the RAF. The following day we took off for Lydda in Palestine (now Israel). We flew along the coast of Libya at about 5000 feet in bright sunlight with good visibility. On the port side we could look down on the blue waters of the

Mediterranean lapping the shore and on the starboard side we could see all the wreckage of the desert campaign. Tanks, vehicles, guns. All left rotting. There were hundreds of crosses marking graveyards, a visible reminder of the waste of war. We flew over El Alamein, that famous battle ground of WWII. In places the flight was a very bumpy one, caused by cool air coming in from the sea and the heat rising from the desert and creating turbulence. In fact it was so rough at one stage that one of the air gunners was sick, the only time I have known an aircrew air sick. I found it a most interesting flight, seeing clearly from the air all the aftermath of the desert campaign which only two years or so previously had dominated the headlines. It was a very historic experience.

After about four and a half hours flying we landed at Lydda, a small pre-war airport and now being used as an RAF staging post. We were to stay here about 36 hours before continuing on the next leg of our journey. We were billeted at a nearby transit camp. It was about 3pm and there was an army truck going into Jerusalem, which we could go on if we wished. We were told that there would be transport back the next morning. Myself and another member of the crew decided to take advantage of this and we got on the truck. We had an uncomfortable ride of about two hours along dusty roads in great heat. The road went along the plains and then up into the hills until we arrived in Jerusalem. After making enquiries we made our way into the old city and booked accommodation for the night at the YMCA hostel, then proceeded to look round the old city with all its historic associations. It was very hot. The streets were very narrow and thronging with people and animals, but we felt we were living in history. We visited the Holy Sepulchre Church and were shown over it by an Orthodox monk. It was very dark inside. It is the main Christian shrine, most of which dates from the time of the Crusades. Inside is the tomb where Christ was laid after he was taken down from the Cross. It is housed in a marble chapel.

In the evening we went into the new town and found a cafe where we had a meal. We witnessed a fight outside the cafe in the course of which one or two were slightly injured. After having eaten we returned to our lodgings in the old city. We each had a bed in a long dormitory. All windows were wide open. They needed to be because it was very hot. For breakfast next morning we had bacon and eggs, which sounds very good but it actually came swimming in fat and combined with the heat I found could not eat it.

After breakfast we gathered the few things which we had taken for the night and made our way to where we were told the transport would be to return to Lydda. We had to wait a while before it came and we began to worry as to whether it would turn up at all and what would happen to us if take off had to be delayed because two members of the crew were missing! However, it did turn up, and we made the return journey arriving back at lunch time and in fact we had a couple of hours or more to wait until we could take off. So we spent an hour or so on the veranda of the airport building watching aircraft taking coming and going. We waited until several other Liberators and their crew were ready to take off, as there were several aircraft going out, and the idea was that were to keep together.

We took off from Lydda and flew to Shaiba in the Persian Gulf, where we landed just as daylight was beginning to fade. A sandstorm was just beginning to make landing tricky. Soon after we landed the airfield closed down, because of the sandstorm, and an aircraft coming into land only just made it. We stayed overnight. It was a wartime airfield used mainly as an RAF staging post on the way to India, uncomfortable and surrounded by desert. We were glad to leave the next day when we took off for Karachi, soon flying over high mountains rising up 9,000 feet, before landing at Mauripur, the then airfield for Karachi. We had accommodation for one night at the airfield. It was tented accommodation and quite comfortable. Then, on the following day, I bade farewell to the crew and wished them luck. They were to pick up a flight engineer as part of a new crew and join a squadron in India to continue the war in the Far Eat against the Japanese while my job was to return to Dorval. This time on my own. They all looked a little forlorn and apprehensive and envious of me of me returning to Canada. I got a seat on an RAF passenger Liberator and returned to the UK with stops for refuelling at Shapur, Cairo, Malta and then to Lyneham in Wiltshire. From Lyneham I travelled to Prestwick by train and then by BOAC to Montreal. Another interesting trip completed which turned out to be my last but one. I was getting used to travelling around the world.

Taking advantage of my five days leave due to me after a trip to India I decided to take another short holiday in the Laurentian mountains. I had gone there during the winter and enjoyed the skiing. Summer time was also great for holidays in the mountains. The weather is continuously hot and there are mountain lakes and the scenery is very attractive. The travel agency recommended that I stay at a guest house beside one of the lakes. I took their advice and took the train. The house was a large one situated beside the lake and run by the owner, a retired business man, and his wife. It was his home but being retired they took in paying guests to supplement their income. Apart from myself there was an elderly couple staying there and a young couple, all, of course, Canadian. The elderly couple left on the second day leaving myself and the young couple as the only guests. The owner had a boat with an outboard motor which he allowed us to use as we wished, provided we paid for the petrol. So we spent a day touring the lake and fishing. There was a very small village nearby with a hotel where we went for a drink in the evening. After a few days the young couple left and so for the last two days of my holiday I had it all to myself. It was a most enjoyable few days and I was sorry when it was over.

THE BEGINNING OF THE END

Chapter Eighteen

On returning to Montreal with the war nearing its end things were beginning to quieten down. Less aircraft were being delivered and I had little to do. I went to the airport most days but sometimes just telephoned to see if I was wanted. It was now late July and very hot and humid in Montreal. I went swimming in the YMCA pool and often at the week end I was invited out to the Montreal sailing club which was situated on the banks of the St Lawrence river, a short distance outside Montreal. It was a lovely place with lawns stretching down to the river. There was dinghy sailing on the river which at Montreal was very wide and for the first time I was able to try my hand at sailing. On Saturday nights there was dancing and supper on the lawn. It was there that I had corn on the cob for the first time with liberal helpings of butter, and probably used as much butter at one meal as the ration for a whole month at home.

At the end of July I made my last trip, which was to deliver a Liberator to Prestwick. On arrival at Prestwick I was told that I would be required as flight engineer to fly a Lancaster back to Canada. I was told I could have a few days leave after which I was to report to an RAF station near Nottingham to meet my crew and pick up the Lancaster which had to be flown back to Canada. For my leave I went and joined Rica and her family who were on holiday in Hoyelake in Cheshire, and had a few days by the sea. After the hot dry and humid weather in Montreal the weather by contrast in Hoyelake was cool and wet. Very British. It was while at Hoyelake that we heard that the first atom bomb had been dropped on Hiroshima.

My leave over I journeyed by train to Nottingham and then to the RAF station near Nottingham where I met my crew. The skipper, an American, was an experienced airline pilot who in the course of his career had flown many types of aircraft but never a Lancaster. He now had to fly one for the first time across the Atlantic. The wireless operator, also a civilian, and the navigator was RAF and myself. In the officers mess that evening was Group Captain Cunningham the night fighter ace.

The following day we flew up to Prestwick where we refuelled and spent the night before taking off, the following day returning to Dorval via Newfoundland. Being summer time the weather conditions over the Atlantic were good. In winter when conditions were bad Lancasters and Mosquitoes were sometimes lost due to ice forming on the wings. These aircraft did not have the efficient de-icing equipment with which the American aircraft, like the Liberator, were equipped. On arriving back at Dorval we heard that a second atom bomb had been dropped on Japan and that Japan had surrendered. Again there was rejoicing and chaos. Not quite to the extent as that which had taken place back in May when Germany surrendered.

The war now over things quietened down. Few aircraft were needed in the various theatres of war and the amount of ferrying reduced considerably. By the end of August ferrying had almost dried up. Such as there was mainly consisted in bringing aircraft back, ferrying in reverse as it were. I did no more trips and the only flying I did was the occasional air test which usually lasted about an hour. I went up to the airport most days to see if I was needed and spent the rest of my time enjoying the sunshine, swimming and socialising at the Air Force club. A pilot friend of mine was posted to the Azores to do a milk round, not on a bicycle but by delivering it daily by aeroplane from the main island, to the nearby dozen or so smaller islands. People were being posted home to the UK during August and September while others like myself were left to have an easy time.

Towards the end of September I received notice of posting. I was to leave early in October. As soon as I informed my parents that I was coming home my mother wrote to me reminding me that at home clothing was rationed and that I ought to get myself stocked up with clothing such as shirts and underwear before I left. Therefore a day or two before leaving I went into one of the large stores in Montreal and bought underpants, vests and shirts, to pack into my case. At the end of the first week in October, almost exactly a year to the day when I had arrived in Canada, I returned to the UK this time by plane not boat. On arriving at Prestwick I was given a rail warrant and told to report to Head Quarters Transport Command Bushey Park Teddington Middlesex. I arrived there after travelling overnight from Prestwick to find a lovely English autumn day, bright and a bit frosty, with the trees beginning to get their autumn colours. After the usual round of routine visits to the medical officer and others I was told I was to report to RAF Riccall in Yorkshire, not far from home. The contrast between the life I had enjoyed for the past year and life from now on became very clear. An atmosphere of austerity soon became manifest, food rationing, clothing rationing and petrol rationing and shortages in every walk of life. Although the black out restrictions had been lifted everything was dull compared to the bright lights of Montreal. I was able to go home for a few days before I had to report to Riccall.

Following a few days leave I reported to RAF Riccall near Selby. A war time bomber station which was in the process of closing down. A Nissan hutted war time camp it was not comfortable but it had the advantage for me in that it was close to home. After two or three weeks the whole station moved to Dishforth, a well built and well appointed pre war station situated alongside the A1 north, a few miles north of Boroughbridge. This had been a Canadian bomber station during the war and was changing over to become a Transport

Command conversion unit to train bomber crews, mainly pilots and flight engineers, for Transport Command. These were now needed for various transport duties, in particular to fly troops and other service personnel home from the middle and far east. We were equipped with Liberators and Yorks and I was to be an instructor. Yorks were a civilian version of the Lancaster bomber. This was a different type of flying. Instead of long haul flights across the Atlantic and across continents this was local flying, and flying in a RAF atmosphere, again. Familiarisation flights, circuits and bumps and an occasional cross country. It was interesting to me to be flying over familiar territory as we regularly flew over Leeds, Harrogate, Scarborough and York. All places I knew well but had never seen from the air before.

Life at Dishforth was pleasant. The flying schedule was by no means excessive as the war being over there were plenty of aircrew available. The station itself was comfortable, sports facilities were good and there were plenty of country pubs in the area. Also I was reasonably near home and I acquired an old Austin ten. Although petrol was rationed it was always possible to scrounge extra and so I was able to get home quite frequently, particularly at week ends.

I was at Dishforth from the end of October 1945 until August 1946 when I came off flying. I was given an administrative job until I was demobilised in January 1947. In true air force fashion at the end of June, within six weeks of coming off flying and within 6 months of being demobilised, I was sent with a few other flight engineers to Manchester for a weeks course at the Avro factory to learn all about the Lancaster, followed by a week at the Rolls Royce factory at Derby to learn all about the Rolls Royce Merlin engine. Having done a tour on Bomber Command, being on Transport Command and this followed by nine months as and instructor, to go on a course to learn all about what I had been doing for the past four years six months before demobilisation did not seem the best use of tax payers money.

CHAIRBORN

Chapter Nineteen

On returning to Dishforth I did very little flying until the beginning of August when I was posted to group headquarters at Heslington Hall, York, as assistant adjutant. Heslington Hall was a lovely Elizabethan Mansion which had been taken over by the RAF at the beginning of the war and used as group HQ.

A lot of beautiful panelling had been stripped to be replaced by plaster board to convert many of the stately rooms into offices. I shared a small office just inside the main entrance with the Adjutant and together we shared the administrative work of the HQ. The adjutant left upon his demobilisation after a few weeks whereupon I was left to do the work of both of us until his replacement was posted in some weeks later. Once again I was close to home and as the head quarters closed at the week end I was able to go home every Saturday and Sunday. After more than three years of continuous flying it was a big change to be in an administrative job. Here I stayed until the beginning of January 1947 when my release came through and I left to collect my gratuity and my issue of civilian clothes. A few days later I started my Economics course at Leeds University and so began a new chapter in my life.

Ray Worrall, September 1989
In the Forest of Freteval
There is no trace of the wartime camp

ICI
VÉCURENT
SAUVÉS PAR LA
RESISTANCE
152
AVIATEURS
ALLIES
MAI-AOUT 1944

Rica and Ray, September 1989
At the Freteval Memorial

FRETEVAL FOREST REMEMBERED

Chapter Twenty

For many years Operation Sherwood, as the escape from the Forest was called by MI9, remained an unknown story of the French and Belgian Resistance movement, except to those who had taken part. In 1966 a committee was formed under Omer Jubault, by then retired from the French police, to erect a memorial at the place where my "army" had collected the airmen over 20 years before. Funds were raised to which the RAF Escaping Society and many other organisations contributed. On 11 June 1967 at an official ceremony, Jean de Blomaert and Airey Neave laid wreathes on the grave of Lucien Boussa at Cloyes. He had died suddenly in the Hotel St Jacques at Cloyes in March. He had gone there to make the final arrangements for the ceremony which
was to take place in June.

On the afternoon of 11 June the French Minister "pour Ancien Combatants" unveiled a plain stone column in the shape of an aircraft tail at the edge of the forest with the inscription:

> *"Ici vecurent sauve par la Resistance 152 aviateurs*
> *Allies, Mai-Aout 1944".*

> *Here lived saved by the Resistance 152 allied*
> *airmen May-August 1944."*

I was fortunate enough to be able to attend the ceremony and met Jean de Blomaert, Virginia de Lake, Omer Jumault and others who had risked their lives to keep us hidden in the forest. Virginia was rescued from Ravensbruck at the end of the war by the Americans when she was little more than a living skeleton, but by 1967 when I met her on this occasion she had fully recovered and was in good health. How we had been able to live from May to August 1944 in this region open to patrols of the occupying German forces remains inexplicable.

I count myself fortunate to have been able to be present at the ceremony on 11 June 1967. Members of the RAF Escaping Society, particularly those who had been hidden in the forest, were invited to attend as a group. However there were difficulties in arranging transport but almost at the last minute the RAF offered to provide an aircraft for us which would depart from Northolt at 6pm on Friday 9 June for an airfield near to Chateaudun and would bring us back to Northolt early Sunday evening. At this period I was practising as a barrister from chambers in Leeds and by the time I heard about these arrangements I had accepted a brief to appear in the Matrimonial court at Leeds on Friday 9 June and so there was no way I was going to be able to get to Northolt in time for a 6pm take off. I was all set to be disappointed. I finished in court about 4pm with the case adjourned until Monday. I went straight into a travel agent and came out ten minutes later having booked an early flight from Leeds / Bradford to Heathrow and a flight from Heathrow to Paris. I returned to chambers and telephoned the secretary of the RAF Escaping Society and told her I was coming after all but would be arriving late.

Early Saturday morning my wife, Rica, drove me up to the airport to catch the 7.30am plane. On landing at Heathrow about an hour later I was able to catch the 10am flight to Paris which took about 45minutes. I then took a taxi to the Gare du Nord and bought a ticket to Chateaudun. The secretary of the Escaping Society had arranged for one of the war time helpers to meet me at Chateaudun station and on meeting him I at once recognised him as one who, as a youth in 1944, was one of the guides who brought escaping airmen to the forest. He was now a physical training teacher at a local school. He took me in his car to Cloyes near to where the ceremony was to be held. On the way we stopped at a little church where every Saturday evening at about 5pm a few Resistance meet to say a prayer in memory of their comrades who had been shot.

We then motored on to Cloyes where a room had been provided for me. After a while the rest of the party arrived back from a visit to the Chateaux of the Loire. They had arrived the previous evening from a days visit to the Loire Chateaux, which had been laid on for them, which, of course, I had missed. That evening a dinner was held in Cloyes for the local Resistance and us allied airmen who had been shot down. There were only a few of us present who had actually hidden in the Forest. On Sunday morning we marched to the cemetery to pay our respects and to lay a wreath on the grave of Lucien Boussa, one of the main architects of the escape who had done so much at great personal risk to himself to organise it and run it. It was his idea to hold the ceremony but sadly he died of a heart attack at Cloyes a few weeks previously having gone there to make final arrangements for the occasion.

Following the wreath laying ceremony we went to the War Memorial for a short ceremony after which were entertained to lunch at the Chateau de Montigny-le-Gannelon, about a mile from Cloyes, which over-looks the river Loir. The Loir is a tributary of the famous Loire. There were many official guests present and as it was a lovely day we were able to enjoy drinks on the terrace overlooking the river followed by an excellent lunch in a large marquee.

In the afternoon a Memorial which had been built at the edge of the forest in the shape of an aircraft tail was unveiled by the French Minister for War before a large crowd. After the ceremony we made for the airfield where the RAF Dakota was waiting to take us back to Northolt where we landed an hour later. The last time I had landed at Northholt was in August 1944 when I was flown back from Normandy in an ambulance plane!

It was a weekend full of memories during which I had een able to renew my acquaintance with Airey Neave who, after his own escape from Colditz earlier in the war, was put in charge of organising escapes from the continent in cooperation with the Resistance. I also met Jean de Blommaert, Virginia de Lake, Omar Jubault and others who had played such an important part in the success of the escape from the Forest of Freteval.

From Northolt I got the train to Kings Cross from where I got the Sleeper to Leeds, arriving in Leeds about 7am on Monday morning. I went home, had a wash and some breakfast, and was back in court to continue my case at 10am. A busy and full weekend. I had taken a risk. Fortunately everything went according to plan but if it had not and I had been delayed and not been available to continue my case I should have been in trouble. However there are some things in life one feels one cannot miss, and this was one of those. I am glad that I took advantage of the opportunity to attend.

A DEBT TO REPAY

Chapter Twentyone

The sacrifices made by our helpers was immense and after the war Lord Portal, the then Chief of Air Staff, upon reading of the heroism of these people requested Sir Basil Embry, who himself had escaped, to form a society from among those like myself who had been rescued, hidden and fed by the Resistance. The object was to help those who had assisted members of The Royal Air Force in their hour of need. In other words to repay the debt which we all knew we owed to them.

In 1946 a meeting was convened at Bush House in London and the Royal Air Force Escaping Society was formed. Since that time until 1995 when the Society was officially wound up the slender resources of the Society were used to help those helpers and their dependents who had fallen on hard times. How did we do it? One of the ways in which we helped was to send money to those of our wartime helpers. For example in the case of a woman, whose husband had been shot in front of her by the Gestapo for sheltering an airman, had grown infirm. She was living in poverty. We were able to send her money and continued to do so each Christmas. Again there was the case of a helper living in Liege who could no longer pursue his trade due to a physical and mental disability resulting from his stay in Buchenwald. We were able to help in a small way, again financially. If it was money that would help we would send it, but never in large sums, to any individual. We tried to spread the limited amount of "butter" available as evenly as possible.

But very often it was help in some practical way rather than financial that was needed. For instance there was a Frenchman who had sheltered a number of airmen and whose daughter, aged 4, was lying gravely ill with meningitis. The French doctor attending her had almost given up hope. He contacted the society and asked if we could help. The child could have been treated in London and the society was prepared to pay the costs, but better still our enquiries led to the discovery that there was a Professor in Paris who was having more success than we were in England with this particular disease. The case was put to him. A bed was made available in the Professors own clinic and as a result the little girl fully recovered. I could go on giving examples of the ways in which we have been able to help over the years, but these examples will suffice.

But help in kind, or financial, did not comprise the whole of our activities. Personal contact was also important and we were able to maintain contact in many ways. Each year for many years in the summer we invited a party of helpers from the continent over here. They were taken to the Royal

Tournament, entertained in RAF messes or at the RAF Club. For many years we held a Christmas party in London and a large number of ex helpers came over for it. Many of us have made visits to the continent, and on many occasions. In the summer of 1982 a Marathon run was arranged in which teams of runners from the Army and the RAF, and some of the more energetic members of the Society, took part. This consisted of a re-run over the old escape route, over a period of 12 days, starting in Belgium and finishing in the Pyrenees from where during the war the airman were taken over the mountains into Spain and then on to Gibraltar.

In 1995 it was decided to wind up the RAF Escaping Society and this was formally done on Battle of Britain Sunday of that year. It was never the intention to go on generation after generation giving help and keeping contact. The intention was to repay our debt by helping our helpers and their children as best we could but not to go beyond that point. The task we set ourselves has been completed and the debt repaid in so far as it has been possible to do so. Of our two standards one has been handed over to the Dean and Chapter of Lincoln Cathedral where it now hangs in the Airman's chapel. The other was handed over to the British Ambassador and hangs in the Embassy in Paris. However as I write the escaping Society is being kept going, on an informal basis, among friends. Thus is drawing to a close a unique bond forged between airmen and their continental helpers arising out of a shared common danger.

Each October members of the Comète escape line hold a reunion in Brussels to which we are invited. We are taken to places of interest, finishing on the Sunday morning with a memorial service in the Basillica at which we pay our respects to the many who died in the course of their activities. This is followed by a lunch. Sadly 2001 was the last such occasion. The Queen of the Belgians attended and my wife and I were delighted to be able to be present. Our friends, like us, feel that the time has come to call it a day for large gatherings. Like us their members are old and like us many of them have passed on. However those of us still able to do so have decided to continue to meet informally each year both here and in Brussels for as long as we are able.

Rica and I have been fortunate enough over the years to have been able to attend many of the events, both in this country and on the continent, and have felt honoured to have met and made friends with many of these brave people. Suffice it to mention a few.

Two names dominate the story of evasion in World War Two. Pat O' Leary (Albert Guerisse) and Andrée (later Comtesse) de Jongh, both Belgian by birth. The Pat O' Leary line was based in Marseille and operated within France. Andrée de Jongh of the postman line later renamed Comète, ran an escape line from Belgium to the Pyrenees and which, from May 1944,

106

included the Forest of Freteval. Both Andrée de Jongh and Pat O' Leary were betrayed and sent to concentration camps. By a miracle and their own will and strength of character they survived. After their arrests both lines reformed and continued to operate until the liberation. In the three years the Comète line returned over 800 aircrew back to England. The cost was staggering. Among helpers captured many were executed and many others never returned from the concentration camps. Both lines were broken many times but were always
rebuilt and continued to operate.

Andrée de Jongh (Dedée) was born in Brussels during the first world war. In 1940 she trained as a nurse. Working in Brussels with the wounded British and Allied soldiers she sought safe houses for them once they were able to walk. She recruited fellow nurses, school friends and anti Nazi Belgians. In August 1941 she arrived at the British Consulate in Bilbao with her first group of four evaders. On arrival she demanded money to pay mountain guides, safe-housekeepers and for food and rail fares. She promised to bring out more evaders in return. She made it clear that the line was Belgian and was to remain so. Dedée organised the line through a system of courriers who moved evaders from one safe house to another right down to the Pyrenees, travelling by bicycle, train and on foot. She took over 150 aircrew to safety in Spain and made the return crossing over the Pyrenees thirty six times. Particularly in winter the route was very difficult and dangerous with the added problem of the fast flowing river Bidassoa in the mountains which had to be crossed.

On 15th January 1943 while sheltering in the final safe house before crossing the Pyrenees Dedée was arrested with her evaders and the safe house-keeper. Someone had betrayed them. Interrogated by the Gestapo Dedée admitted she was the leader of the Comète line. The Gestapo at first did not believe her thinking that such a young girl could not possibly be the leader. She was taken back to Brussels for further questioning. When it became apparent to the Gestapo that they would get nothing out of her she was sent to Ravensbruck concentration camp to simply disappear. She was interrogated daily for twelve months. Enquiries about her fate from friends and family met with silence. Conditions were horrific. After a diet of potato and turnip soup for two years and using her nursing knowledge to assist herself and the other prisoners she was released at the end of the war. Her mother who had also been imprisoned was also released but her father was burnt to death when his concentration camp was set alight by the retreating Germans. Dangerously ill when released she recovered and then worked for many years in a leper colony in the Congo and later, when civil war broke out there, she took charge of a leper hospital in Ethopia. After many years she retired to Brussels. She was awarded the George Medal after the war and later made a Countess by the King of the Belgians. My wife and I were fortunate to be at the Comète luncheon in Brussels when this took place. She also received French and Belgian decorations.

One of the evaders arrested with her in January 1943 was Stan Hope, a Mosquito navigator/radio operator. After the arrest he was also interrogated by the Gestapo and then sent to a POW camp for the rest of the war. After the war he and his wife ran a business in Ireland. However a few years ago they retired and came to live in Leeds, by coincidence about a mile from where I live. Subsequently I met him by chance and I now see him frequently. In spite of the deprivations of a POW camp all those years ago he is, at 87, fit and well. In October 2001 my wife and I went to the last of the Comète reunions in Brussels. Stan came with us where he met Andrée de Jongh (now in her 80's and very frail. This was the first time they had seen each other since their arrest by the Gestapo in 1943. A happy occasion after so many years. If he and I had not met by chance a few years ago this would never have happened.

Andrée Antoine Dumon (code name Nadine) was one of the original couriers with Andrée de Jongh (Dedée) and her father Frederick de Jongh who had started the Comète line in Brussels in the dark days of 1940/41. As the line progressed, Nadine became the right arm of both Dedée and her father in Brussels and in Paris. Initially responsible for the setting up of the line from Brussels to Paris and with her sister Michou she collected evaders in Brussels and took them to Paris. At times the men were taken via Corbie where the river Somme had to be crossed to avoid border controls. Later Nadine took evaders from Paris to the Western Pyrenees, mainly by train, for crossing into Spain. The Dumon family were fully involved with the Comète line. Both daughters were couriers and Father and Mother were involved in the line in Brussels.

Nadine was arrested on 11 August 1942 together with her parents. Michou, still free took over Nadine's role and continued taking evaders over the Pyrenees. The Gestapo thought that they had captured Andrée de Jongh the leader of Comète as they shared the same Christian name and were similar in size. Nadine was treated badly in prison and interrogated daily for twelve months. Finally when the Germans decided that they could get no more information from her she was sent to the appalling conditions of Ravensbruck, North of Berlin, and after that to Mauthausen, until released by the Allies. Nadine returned to Brussels very ill. Her mother had also been released but her father was murdered by the Nazis.

Typically Comète once again reorganised after the war and formed the Comète Reunion association, of which Nadine became the secretary. She was awarded the MBE.

Micheline Dumon (now Ugeux, whose code name was Michou) is the sister of Andrée (Nadine). She had been involved with Comète from the beginning and at 19 was one of the lines first helpers. Michou organised the collection and despatch of evaders in Paris. When her sister was arrested on 11 August she took over the work of leading evaders over the Pyrenees. Between December 1943 and May 1944 she took ten men over the Pyrenees. When her father and mother were arrested in March 1944 in Paris along with a number of other helpers, including a woman dentist, Michou was convinced that there was a traitor in the line. The method which she adopted to find the name of the traitor was characteristic of her extraordinary bravery. She went to the notorious Fresnes prison in Paris and stood outside the walls from where she could observe the women's quarters. She did not know the position of the cell where the woman dentist named Martine was imprisoned but she shouted Martine, Martine, and Martine's voice answered. Michou called again who betrayed you. Faintly from inside the prison walls the answer came back "it was Pierre Boulain". The Resistance showed no mercy to traitors.

Hunted by the Gestapo, Michou continued to outwit them and finally escaped by the skin of her teeth when in May 1944 with the Gestapo on her trail she crossed the Pyrenees with a group of evaders and came to England. On her arrival in England she volunteered for work with the SOE and to be dropped back into France. The war finished before she could be parachuted back. After the war she was awarded the MBE and George Medal, along with French and Belgian decorations.

Raymond Itterbeek was born in Brussels on October 19th 1922. Raymond was a 17 year old student and boy scout leader when his country was invaded in the spring of 1940. At the age of 18 he joined the Belgian Resistance. His father and mother were already members. In 1942 they hid two Jewish families. One, a family of four who survived, the other a family of eight, who were arrested and deported and disappeared. Raymond was also actively involved with a number of clandestine organisations including the secret army, known as the "service zero", the Movement National Belge, and in the underground press which printed and distributed "illegal" newspapers. He was also involved in armed clashes with collaborators and the forces of occupation.

At the beginning of 1943 Raymond joined the Comète Escape line organisation which was loosing many of its couriers and safe house-keepers as a result of infiltration by the Gestapo, and the German intelligence. When he first joined Comète he was told about the dangers and if he was lucky that he may be able to remain active for three months before capture. Then he could expect torture and death, or at best a concentration camp. He was also asked that, should he be captured, to hide his identity and to pass on no information for 48 hours. This would allow Comète to reorganise. His job with

Comète was finding safe houses for aircrew evaders who were collected in them and taken down the line, then over the Western Pyrenees, going on to Gibraltar. Although he controlled seven safe houses in Brussels he also acted as a courier escorting evaders from Brussels to Paris and then through France.

On 3rd January 1944 Raymond was arrested on the train to Lille with two British evaders, both Wing Commanders. Detained by the Abwehr (the German counter espionage system) he was sent to Loos prison. The two airmen were sent to a POW camp. Despite harsh interrogation and torture Raymond did not reveal his true name and identity for three weeks. This delay enabled Comète to clear all of Raymond's safe houses and to warn all contacts to go to ground. His parents had also been arrested for Resistance activities and both had been condemned to death. His sister Elaine left the family home and sought refuge with other safe house-keepers and remained free and continued her work with Comète. After the war she married an Englishman and together they ran a pub in the South of England. I met her with her husband a few years ago in Stratford-upon-Avon. They were then living in retirement at Ludlow.

Sentenced to death in Brussels on 27th August 1944 Raymond was moved with about 30 other members of Comète who had been captured in Brussels and Paris. These included his friends Jean Francois Northomb (code name Franco), and Jacques Le Grelle (Jerome), and Albert Mattens (Jean-Jacques). Franco had been leader of Comète after Andrée de Jongh (Dedée). Many former safe house-keepers were also in the group. All were deported to concentration camps in Germany. Raymond's father had also been deported and his mother had been sent to the concentration camp at Ravensbruck. Raymond's group were actually quite fortunate in being sentenced to death because it meant they remained prisoners in the hands of the German army and not the hated SS The army still retained a sense of discipline and obeyed orders and fortunately no order ever came through for Raymond to be executed. If the SS had been in charge of the prisoners it is almost certain that they would have been killed. The SS had no rules. They executed and tortured people whenever and however they liked. In the summer of 1945 American troops liberated the camp in which Raymond was held. He was later reunited with his mother and father who had also survived and his sister who had remained free.

All these people have regularly attended the reunions in Belgium and England and Rica and I have been honoured and humbled to have met them and counted them as our friends. For

The lives of brave men (and women)
shall all remind us,
that we can make our lives sublime
and in departing leave behind us
footprints in the sands of time.

Adapted from H W Longfellow (1807 - 82)

And so at the end of the day I ask myself what if the situation had been reversed and we had been occupied by a foreign power. Would I have done what they did? Would I have given food and shelter at the risk of torture or death to a complete stranger whose language I could not speak and in all probability would never see again?

In all honesty I have to say I am not sure.

Raymond Worrall
Allandale
Alwoodley
Leeds

April 2004

On the occasion of the 50th
anniversary of the liberation of
Belgium

the Amicale Comète

wishes to recognize the courage and zeal
in combat during the 1939-1945 war, of

Raymond Worrall

as well as the loyalty and friendship
he has shown to the Amicale Comète
over the past 50 years

La Présidente
Comtesse Andrée De Jongh

Le Vice-Président
Jean-François Nothomb

Secrétaire
Andrée Antoine-Dumont

Trésorier
Raymond Itterbeek

23/10/1994.

Sources and Acknowledgements

Books

Bomber Command Losses 1994

Saturday at MI9 by Airey Neave

No 5 Group Bomber Command RAF by W J Laurence

Pilots and Flight Engineers Notes – Air Publication 2062A

MI9 Escape and Evasion 1939-45

A Midsummer Nights Dream by Ken Andrews

Green Markers Ahead Skipper by Gilbert Gray

Acknowledgements

First my thanks to my wife Fredrica without whose encouragement this book would not have been written, and for the support and interest which she has shown by attending with me over many years the numerous functions and events of the RAFES, both here and on the continent, sometimes by sacrificing other holidays.

Next my thanks to Air Chief Marshal Sir Lewis Hodges for contributing the foreword, for his careful reading of the text and for taking the trouble to telephone me on several occasions with helpful suggestions and advice. Himself an evader in the early years of the war he subsequently flew with and commanded special duties squadrons and was President of the Royal Air Force Escaping Society until 1995 when it was formally wound up. His assistance is much appreciated.

I also owe my thanks to Colin Sheard who flew as an observer with the Fleet Air Arm during the war and who applied his teaching skills to carefully scrutinise the text, correcting many mistakes and errors. My thanks also go to Elizabeth Harrison, who, for many years until it was wound up, was a most able secretary of the RAFES, for her help and advice. And finally, to my publishers, Silver Quill, who have made this book both possible and affordable.